# The Last of the Giants

# The Last of the Giants

## Harry Rimmer, LL.D.

★ ★ ★ ★ ★ ★

This reprint published by

## Northern Canada Mission Distributors

Every effort has been made to secure permission for this reprint
including a copyright search of The Library of Congress .

ISBN 0–920731–48–1

1992
Printed in Canada

*"There were giants in the earth
in those days."*

Genesis 6:4

To the company of
**THE GIANTS,**
the Apostles of the Pines, whose
spirits were as tall as the trees
beneath which they walked, and
whose hearts were as big as the
vast land they conquered for
God, this book is reverently
dedicated.

"And Elijah took HIS MANTLE, and wrapped it together, and smote the waters, and they were divided hither and thither, so that they two went over on dry ground.

And it came to pass, when they were gone over, that Elijah said unto Elisha, Ask what I shall do for thee, before I be taken away from thee. And Elisha said, I pray thee, let a double portion of thy spirit be upon me.

And he said, Thou hast asked a hard thing: nevertheless, if thou see me when I am taken from thee, it shall be so unto thee; but if not, it shall not be so.

And it came to pass, as they still went on, and talked, that, behold, there appeared a chariot of fire, and horses of fire, and parted them both asunder; and Elijah went up by a whirlwind into heaven.

And Elisha saw it, and he cried, My father, my father, the chariot of Israel and the horsemen thereof. And he saw him no more: and he took hold of his own clothes, and rent them in two pieces.

He took up also THE MANTLE of Elijah that fell from him, and went back, and stood by the bank of Jordan."

II Kings 2:8-13.

The Rev. Elwin ("Al") Channer
September 1947

# FOREWORD

There *is* such a thing as "Apostolic Succession," and we Protestants are well acquainted with it as it is interwoven in our history and spiritual heritage. I do not mean a mythical and mystical transmission of power from Peter, who was never in Rome and who died centuries before there was a pope, but to the New Testament form of apostolic succession. When Jesus chose the Twelve, he stated the purpose of this choice in these words, "Ye shall be witnesses of me." No apostle was ever called to sit on an earthly throne in the pride of splendor to rule with arrogance over the humbler children of God. They were called to go forth and adventure their lives to make Christ known among lost men.

When Paul was near the end of his course he gazed with pride on a young man, who was strong in the faith and learned in the Word, knowing that his ministry would continue in Timothy. To this stalwart he wrote at least two epistles, commending Timothy for his fidelity to the faith, and setting forth certain counsels which would aid him in preserving the purity of the revelation given through the Apostle Paul. In like manner, as each of the others went to their rest, they could look with gratitude upon a host of converts, all witnesses to the saving power of Christ, and among whom there were some who were capable of carrying on the work which the original apostles, had so nobly begun. This is *true* "apostolic succession."

A classical illustration is found in the history of the prophet Elijah. When he reached the end of his career and was awaiting translation, his lieutenant went with him to the home-going of the great prophet. When Elijah asked the young Elisha what parting gift he desired, the acolyte asked for a double portion of the Spirit which had been upon his master. To this Elijah replied that he was unable to grant such a request, but that the gift would be given if Elisha saw the passing into glory of his master.

When Elijah was gone, Elisha took up and wore the mantle of the prophet, and the power of God followed him. When the sons of the prophets saw him coming they saluted him as the heir to power, because he wore the mantle.

In the great north woods of Minnesota, God called a mighty man to be the first Apostle of the Pines. Of this man you have read, and some of his story is given in these following pages. When the new work was begun, this leader, Frank Higgins, gathered about him other spiritual giants and they stormed the ramparts of evil for God. They became known as "the apostles of the pines," although the lumberjacks called them "Sky Pilots." The heart and genius of the work was Higgins, who died at an early age, killed by his labours for the Lord.

No work of God can end until He is ready to close it, so when Higgins died his mantle fell upon a converted outlaw, John Sornberger. In time he also was gathered to the company of the Blessed, and the mantle then descended to a third man, Elwyn Channer, who wears it with distinction and honour to this present day.

This is *real* "apostolic succession!" One man wins another to Christ, that one wins a score more, and they in turn bear fruit for God in their testimony and ministry. So back to Paul, through Timothy, we who preach Christ can trace a proud and noble spiritual heritage, from which we should draw strength and inspiration, being sure that the line of succession will not end with us.

This is a book about men of this descent. Spiritual giants who walked with huge strides across a majestic land. Their task was colossal and their enemies as powerful as Satan himself, but they were great enough to prevail. Most of these men I knew. With some of them I have roamed these woods fishing, hunting, and preaching in the camps where their ministry extended. I present them to you as men who are entitled to shining crowns they won by their gargantuan endeavors for God!

# List of Illustrations

# Table of Contents

## BOOK ONE

THE SKY PILOT

## BOOK TWO

THE BULL OF THE WOODS

## BOOK THREE

THE LAST OF THE GIANTS

Frank Higgins — The Original Sky Pilot

# BOOK ONE

## The Sky Pilot

# The Northern Genesis

# CHAPTER I

# The Northern Genesis

The roots of many American cities reach far back into history to tap the well-springs of romance, but none has a more gripping appeal to the student of our national beginnings than Duluth, Minnesota. Its history goes back before the Revolution, and the *voyageurs* who sought a watery highway to China knew the site before the colonies were established in New England. From the waters of the St. Lawrence these men had adventured westward in their desire to link China and France by way of the western world, and they paddled and toiled from lake to lake seeking the point where the sweet waters merged with the salty tides of the Pacific Ocean. In September of 1634 Jean Nicolet passed through the Straits of St. Mary to stand on the eastern shore of Lake Superior, feeling confident that in its broad expanse he had found the western ocean. Nicolet had lived for 16 years among the Indians, who dwelt by the shores of the lakes and in the deep forests that marched away from their banks, and he had learned their lore as well as he had mastered their languages. So certain was this intrepid Frenchman that there was a passage to the ocean and hence to China by way of the sweet waters, he carried a court robe with him on his voyages of discovery, so that he could fittingly represent his king when he was at last in the presence of the Emperor of China.

As far as records go, Nicolet was only the second white man who set eyes on Lake Superior. He had been preceded ten years before by the young explorer Etienne Brule, who, while living among the Hurons, had journeyed with them to the Straits and had viewed the crystal waters of the most northern of the unsalted seas. So thoroughly did Brule accommodate himself to the life of his red brethren that he became a savage, and was postscribed as a traitor to France by Champlain. Utterly indifferent to European opinion he became completely Indian in his ideals and conduct, and lived as a savage until he was slain and eaten by his adopted kinsmen, the Hurons. It is a tragedy that he did not preserve his relations with Champlain as did the other *voyageurs*, since we would then have had his memoirs and records to enlarge our knowledge of the history of those early times.

The discovery of Lake Superior led to the finding of the Mississippi River, and for a time China was forgotten while the tide of exploration turned south. The suspicion was born in the minds of these great French adventurers that the huge inland waters went on to infinity, and that there was no "head of the lakes." Indian legends peopled the fabulous far shores with strange races, and they talked of islands that eyes could not see across. So it was when Marquette set out on his renowned voyage. After weeks of hazardous travel, he came along the north shore to the mouth of the St. Louis River. Crossing the sand spit that is now named Minnesota Point, which separates Duluth from Superior, he gazed on the bay and the St. Louis. In wonder and delight he cried, "Fond du lac!" and the head of the lakes had been reached. Up the St. Louis he voyaged to Lake Itasca, where the Father of Waters is born, and down the Mississippi to write his name large upon the scroll of fame.

The fur traders of the Astor Company set up a post at Fond du Lac in 1825, and by 1830 it had grown to a population of 1,750 men. This might be called the beginning of the present city of Duluth, whose fortunes have fluctuated from one extreme to the other in time with the discovery and exhaustion of one source of treasure after another. Fur was only the beginning, but it was a rich and startling one. A single season saw 184,150 pelts go out of the new post at the "Head of the Lakes," and among them were some of the most valued of the furred treasures. Beaver, of course, headed the list with more than a hundred thousand skins. Thirty-two thousand marten skins and seventeen thousand muskrat hides helped swell the total, and forty-six hundred otter pelts enriched the traders in that one shipment.

When the rich deposits of fur were depleted, the minds of the adventurers turned to the thought of copper. The Indians claimed that there was a solid boulder of copper near the mouth of the Ontonagon River, which was a sacred object to some of the tribes. In 1667, a Jesuit missionary saw and recorded copper deposits in the bed of this steam, so the legends of the Indians seemed to be founded upon fact. A century after this priest had told his tale, a fur trader named Alex Henry had been guided to the same spot by the Indians, when he expressed curiosity about their copper ornaments and arrowheads. He saw the boulder and hacked off a piece with a tomahawk, and estimated its weight at about ten tons.

Other trappers and traders visited the boulder, and in 1819, Henry Schoolcraft, the famed scholarly Indian Agent, saw and surveyed the object. His report to Washington is on file, and he said it was copper in a very pure state, and highly valuable.

In 1843, a Michigan prospector bought the boulder from the Indians, and skidded and rolled it down to the mouth of a stream where he had a schooner anchored to transport it. He was halted by the Federal agents who claimed it as government property, and tried to seize it from him. He paid the U. S. Government $1,365.00 for possession, and again started to lighter it to the ship. This time the War Department tried to grab it, and while they wrangled, the man, whose name was Eldred, got his treasure aboard and slipped away.

Arriving safely in Detroit after arduous labour and surviving many hazards, he placed the fabled object on view in a museum where throngs paid to see it. But his troubles were not over. In spite of the bill-of-sale he had from the Federal agents, which was perfectly valid, the Government again seized it and took it to Washington; this time for the Smithsonian Institution, where it now reposes far from its place of origin. Four years later the Government compensated Eldred to the amount of a little over $5,600. He considered himself lucky to get *that* much, so he took it and said no more.

A year after Eldred started to move his huge nugget, copper mining began in earnest on the North Shore. The ventures were financed almost entirely by Boston capital, and these companies reaped a rich harvest in the subsequent years. Fond du Lac continued to send out its diminishing streams of fur, but copper for a time became the chief source of income.

While the red metal was still at the height of its production, a government surveyor reported that he had such trouble with the needle of his compass spinning he could not run a true line. He investigated, he said, and discovered a large outcropping of pure iron, whose influence was so strong the compass could not be made to function, and he described the location and size of the deposit.

His report was filed as an interesting but not important document, and nothing more was done about it. But a man named Philo Everett heard of this document, and made a prospecting trip which left him wildly excited. He gathered his resources and opened the deposit, and the famous Marquette Range was developed and its wealth flowed out to the coffers of the growing nation.

In the year 1854 there were just seven shanties on the present site of Duluth, and Fond du Lac was still the important post. But a driving, restless prospector and adventurer named George Stuntz heard a rumour of a new iron range at Lake Vermilion. He made an exhaustive survey, and, convinced that a fortune was to be had for the taking, he went to Philadelphia and met the financial adventurer, Jay

Cooke. Entranced by the stories that Stuntz told him, Mr. Cooke made the long journey to the North Country and saw the deposit. He became as enthused as Stuntz was, put his money behind the venture and the Vermilion Range was opened up.

Duluth began to boom, and a city sprang up almost overnight. Fond du Lac was all but forgotten. Timber only was used to build the mushroom town, and adventurers, miners, prospectors, and settlers poured in as fast as ships, canoes, teams, and trains could bring them. Every sort of business prospered. The city organized and planned for the future. Docks were constructed, streets laid out, and the boom boomed on at a merry pace. Then came the panic of 1873, and Jay Cooke was wiped out. In his gigantic failure the city joined, and the collapse was so colossal Duluth became practically a ghost town. The footloose fled the scene. Such merchants as could salvage the price of a journey left for better fields, and weeds grew in the new streets.

Hurt, but not out, George Stuntz returned to Philadelphia and interested another financier, Charlemagne Tower. Intrigued by the prospect of an iron empire, Tower backed Stuntz with his millions, and the wheels began to turn again. The Duluth and Iron Range Railroad was built from Vermilion to Two Harbours, where loading docks were constructed to load the ore on boats. Although the railroad did not come within a score of miles of Duluth, the city shared the general prosperity which followed, and began to move ahead.

Because municipal bonds paid a high rate of interest and were easy to sell, the city had financed its development by the sale of such bonds. They became due, the crash had left the city broke, and there was no money to pay the indebtedness. Things were so black at one time that the newly-elected city officials refused to qualify and take the oath of office. This left the bondholders with no legally responsible person on whom they could serve legal papers and summons. Affairs

23

were at a stalemate. Then a plan of compromise was arranged whereby the investors were guaranteed some salvage from their investment, and the city began to function again.

The grain from the Dakotas began to pour down into the city for shipment to the East and to Europe. Huge elevators were constructed, and money flowed like water. The progress of the city was steady from that time on. The unbelievably rich Mesaba Iron Range was discovered and developed, and Duluth became the loading point for the shipment of that ore. It was 1892 before the first load of Mesaba iron was shipped to the smelter in Cleveland, but that was the dawn of a new era for a vast region. Producing more ore in a given time than all the other ion sources of the nation combined, the Mesaba made millionaires out of men who had been labourers and brought ease and comfort to multiplied thousands.

When Duluth was founded, the hills upon which she stands were covered with great tracts of huge, straight Norway pines. The site of the city provided the lumber for the construction of the new homes. When other sources of wealth failed or fluctuated, the timber was always there. Suddenly operators awoke to the fact that the Michigan woods were all but depleted. Saginaw was done as a lumber center, and the big operators turned to Minnesota with its untouched forests that stretched for hundreds of miles. Like a horde of consuming locusts the barons and their legions descended, and the rape of a new region was on.

It was an age of gigantic action, and the men whom fiction writers and biographers are fond of referring to as "Empire Builders" were ruthless robbers of the public domain and thieves of the nation's treasures. Had any supervised system of logging been initiated at the beginning, the woods of Minnesota could have provided an abundance of lumber for a thousand years. But they looted the land for a quick profit, and they squandered our heritage for sudden wealth. They took out only the biggest and best trees, and slashed or burned the rest. And of the big trees they often took only the clear part, the one-third which extended from the stump to where the branches began to jut out. The rest they burned. Cedar, not so large or valuable as pine, they destroyed in their haste. It would be worth a thousand fortunes today.

To start with, they stole the lands. The Government had declared much of the forest in Minnesota "Stone and Timber Claims" and a citizen could take up 160 acres by filing on it. The big operators would hire a cruiser to survey the best stands of timber and draw up a description of the boundaries. Then they would give a lumberjack ten dollars and a quart of whiskey to go to the land office and file on that claim. The jack would then deed the claim to the operator, who thus got a hundred thousand dollars worth of timber for ten dollars, a quart of whiskey, and a little quiet perjury!

This, of course, was quite in keeping with the customs of "Big Business" in those days. Here is a typical illustration of the methods of these "Empire Builders," and one of the effects of their actions upon the region today. You may know that highway 46 passes through the Chippewa National Forest, and that for many miles it runs as straight as a string. When you drive south on this highway, you are sighted on the water tower of Deer River for a long straight run. The reason is this:

The Canadian National Railroad desired a right-of-way into Duluth from Winnipeg to facilitate the shipment of wheat. They bought the necessary rights, surveyed the road, and cut and cleared the roadbed from Duluth to the Canadian border. At that psychological moment, unfortunately, Jim Hill decided he needed a link to tie his lines together and bind the east and the west. But he was just too late. The Canadian National already had the line started on the only route he could use.

Before radio was invented, these great financiers had the legislatures "wired for sound." That is, they pulled the wires and the legislators made the proper sounds! The Hill interests got very patriotic, and had a law passed prohibiting any railroad from passing through any national forest, on the grounds that the sparks from the locomotives might set fires and destroy the national resources. Since a portion of the new right-of-way passed through the Chippewa Forest, the Canadian National was stymied and had to stop building. So Hill bought their interests for ten cents on the dollar, used the part he needed for a railroad, and sold the rest for a highway to the border! The Canadian National, some years later, had to find a route down the North Shore and come into Duluth that way.

So the timber barons were just in step with their times. They stole the acreage, they looted the forests, they drove men like beasts, but they made money! And when a region was devastated they swept on to fresh fields. Of course, there were decent men among them; men who deplored the conditions and tried to better them. But the competition was keen, and skull-duggery was the order of the day, and an operator had to stay ahead or go under. Some of them made millions and died rich. Some of them ended as drunkards, victims of the vile conditions which they helped to bring about.

But when the timbers started falling and the mills began to turn out lumber, Duluth was the natural outlet for the produce, so she reaped a large measure of the golden stream that flowed from the green back country. The raiders began at the ridges that crested the city sky line, and they destroyed the trees all the way to the Canadian border, and in so doing they helped to build and enrich the city by the greatest of the inland seas. Even today caulked boots and mackinaws are a common sight in her streets, but a new generation of lumberjack celebrates in a quiet, orderly way in her tamed and gentled Bowery.

Duluth seems to rise out of the lake, which bathes its foundations in its lower streets. Tier upon tier the city rises as though in retreat from the icy waters and cold blasts of mighty Superior, the houses seeming to float one above the other in a poised position, as though ready to join the flight of the birds who annually turn south. The glittering jewels of the passing ships are matched, multiplied, and magnified by the lights in the orderly rows of illumined homes, or by the twisting, winding necklaces of street lights which line the highways, which in turn follow the contours of the hills. The vista rises from height to height until the top of the lovely city is lost in the deep green of the forests which have sprung up to hide the scars of ancient logging operations, and the initiate knows that miles of muskeg, peat, and "poppel" lead back to the treasure trove of the Mesaba Range. Down from these heights crawl the trains of iron ore, each car laden with its tons of brown-red wealth, to cascade into the holds of the long slim vessels which will bear it to the fiery furnaces of the far east. By night in fair weather the dwellers in the heights can see the lights of the graceful ships as they shuttle up and down on their thousand-mile watery tread-mill, and when fog obscures the view, the mournful and somber blasts of the fog horns signal the passing of the long ships. It is the most romantic and historically-rich city on the American Continent, and to know it is to love it as no other city deserves affection. Those who have felt its power and appeal never forget, and its roaming sons and daughters inevitably return again and again as a prodigal turns toward home.

# Lumber and the Jacks

# CHAPTER II

# Lumber and the Jacks

The almost endless stand of graceful, swaying pines offered a challenge and a bait to the avarice of greedy men, which it was impossible to resist. The forests had remained undisturbed for many centuries when peopled by Indians, but they were doomed from the moment the eyes of money-hungry white men first saw them. The mouths of the looters actually watered at the sight of endless miles of tall pines, five and six feet in diameter, just waiting for the axe and the saw. Rivers and streams crossed and bisected the great forests, making it easy and cheap to transport the fallen giants to a mill and a market, and the land was ripe to plunder.

The legionaries who swept to the fray were a hardy crew, as rough and wild as savages could be. While they were in the woods they lived a life that was different from that in any other environment, and their code of ethics was peculiar to themselves. All through the bitter winter they chopped and sawed, piled and loaded their landings, and when the spring freshets filled the streams bankful, they dumped the accumulation of stacked timber into the flood and drove madly down to their markets. There they were paid off in hard money, and there they met the flock of harpies and sharpers who waited to fleece them of a year's pay, and send them back broke, sick with rotgut booze, and cursing the towns that had robbed them. But the next drive saw them back again, eager to be mulcted of their pay by tavern keepers, lewd women, and crooked gamblers. Their happy-go-lucky philosophy was expressed by a Swede chopper, who came into town after seven months in the woods and collected his pay. He went into the nearest saloon, bought a drink of whiskey, and paid for it from the top of a roll of bills that made the bartender's eyes gleam with avarice. With spurious geniality he said, "Just in town, Ole?" "Yah," said the Swede, "ay bane going to have some fun, ay bat you!" "Sure," said the publican, "and I'll bet you earned it. Have a drink on the house."

Ole smiled his gratitude and took the free drink. A minute or two later he went out like a light. The drink was spiked with knock-out drops. When Ole woke up early next morning he was lying in a back alley with his pockets inside out. He had a head that felt like a blacksmith was using it for an anvil, and a taste in his mouth that would have done credit to a sewer. He struggled to his feet, looked at his empty pockets, and said, "Val, easy come, easy go!" and headed back for the employment office and another half year in the woods. His "easy come" meant fourteen hours of man-killing labour each day for seven months. His "easy go" meant one drink which he enjoyed and one which he did *not!*

Liquor was the curse, but the first recourse of the lumberjack. He had a rare sense of humour that enabled him to laugh at his own troubles and misfortunes. He could turn a joke on any occasion. The saloon was his club, his office, his refuge, and the only place where he felt at home when in town, and the whiskey peddlers were careful to foster this feeling. When the jacks arrived and took over a town, every tavern keeper knew he could count on tens of thousands of dollars before the boys quit and headed back to the camps. Most of them employed tough men and shifty women to rob the men as soon as they were drunk enough, and it was a common custom to set out free drinks of the most potent kind to get the victims unconscious in a hurry, so they could be "rolled" for their wealth.

The names of their favourite drinks were typical of the frontier. They called the various brands of liquor "Tiger Sweat," "Panther Juice," "Hardware," "Man Killer" and plain "Rotgut." The most common name was "Squirrel Whiskey," and legend claims that this name was coined on the Bowery in Duluth. According to the story, a Swede from the camps came up to a bar and said, "Ay vant a bottle of squirrel whiskey." The puzzled bartender said, "Squirrel whiskey? I never heard of it. I can give you a bottle of Old Crow." "No," said the Swede, "ay don't want to fly, ay yust vant to yump around a little!" The name stuck, and any corn-juice potent enough to make a man leap with the shock when it went down his gullet was henceforth known as "squirrel whiskey."

The average employer was utterly ruthless in regard to the men. Wages were low, from fifty cents to a dollar a day, with bed and board. The board was generally good, the beds were unspeakably awful. In the western woods, especially on the Pacific Coast, the word "camp" meant the entire acreage of an operation. There were a number of buildings that went to make up a camp. First and most important was the cook house, the largest building in the camp. One end of it was the kitchen, generally manned by a Chinese crew. (The North woods never saw a Chinese as far as living memory goes) The major part of the "cook house" was the mess hall, where the jacks ate three times a day. It was equipped with long tables and seated with benches. The tables were covered with white oil-cloth. The northern camps were quite innocent of any such frills or folderols, being equipped just with plain pine tables. In the western "camp" there was a saw-filer's shed, a tool house, a company store, which was the social center of the camp, and a large number of bunk houses, generally accommodating from four to eight men.

In the North woods the word "camp" generally meant the bunk house. Here was the shelter and resting place of the jacks, and it was a crude refuge at best. The first and earliest type was called a "muzzle loader," since it had but one opening; the huge front door. The bunks were built out from the walls so that a man slept with his head to the logs and his feet to the center of the camp. They were built one above the other to the height of three bunks, crowding the men into the smallest possible space. In the center was a barrel stove or box stove, a cast-iron device with a fire box so huge it could swallow four-foot lengths of wood. Around the stove the men hung their clothes to dry, and an atmosphere of steaming woolens and sour sweat perfumed the edifice at all times. At the far end of this bunkhouse a grindstone was placed, so that in their spare time the jacks could sharpen their tools. No lumberjack was ever lonesome in such a bed. He generally had *thousands* of company! Bedbugs and cooties were the common and expected rule, and an old-time jack would have regarded a camp that was not infested as an unhealthy place.

The later type of "camp" had the beds parallel to the wall so the occupants were lying the same way the logs were laid. These bunkhouses were an improvement, as they were only two bunks high, and were built only along the sides, allowing the end to be clear. Also, there was a door in each end of the building. This change was brought about by the demand of the state, due to the fire hazard of the older "muzzle loader." When as many as a hundred and eighty men had to fight their way out of the one door of a blazing camp, some of them never reached safety.

In the better camps there were benches called "deacon seats," which the men could use to lounge and rest upon, and where they sometimes played cards or rolled the dice. By the front entrance, on the outside of the bunkhouse, a shelf was built. This was faced with a six-inch board to make a trough, and tin wash basins were placed therein for the more particular who wanted to wash. As for bathing facilities, they were ample. No one ever dreamed of taking a bath! If some original character ever got so fantastic an idea, there was the river or the creek, if he wanted to chop a hole in the ice, soap himself, and get in. About once every two weeks the more sanitary jacks would boil all of their clothes in a fifty pound lard pail over an open fire in the woods, and start all over again. But the bunks were *always* infested, and nobody expected anything different.

In those earlier days one of the Mission Boards sent a missionary up to one of the camps to take a survey, and consider the possibility of evangelizing the men. He was a devout and good man, who had recently graduated from seminary. Someone had warned him about the abundance of personal pets harboured by the jacks, and when the preacher got to the camp he asked the cook if he had a spare bunk that was not inhabited by questionable insects. The cook, who had the perverse sense of humour that was a trait of all lumberjacks, said there was no spare bed, but he would put him in a bunk with a man he could guarantee was clean. Then he put the innocent victim of his practical joke in with the lousiest man in camp, the scaler. After two restless hours the preacher got up and dressed, sat up all the rest of the night, and left by daylight—still scratching!

This sort of humour extended to their games and sports. One of the common customs was to inveigle a greenhorn into a game of "hot hand." A leader would sit down on the deacon seat with a hat in his lap, and the man who was "it" would kneel and put his face down in the hat, with his "southern exposure" prominently displayed. The other boys would get in a half-circle around him and take turns swatting the beam of the man with their huge palms. After each spank the victim would raise up and try to guess who had smacked him. If he guessed right, that man would take his place and the game would go on. When they had a greenhorn in camp they would set the stage by concealing a jack in an upper bunk, with a logger's rubber nailed to a long strip of wood. With the fearsome weapon he could get a swing and land a wallop that would raise a blister. When the poor dupe was lured into the game they would play it honestly and with great hilarity until *he* was down. Then the fun really began. He never guessed who had hit him, of course, since the swatter was concealed in the top bunk, and he stayed "down" until he could hardly get up!

If someone displeased the crowd, they tossed him in a blanket and hurled him into a snow bank. If one of the number violated the code of ethics or broke an unwritten law they gave him one day to get out of camp or get thrown in the river. They were a rude, rough, roistering, brawling, and lusty generation, and the earth knows their kind no more.

All winter long they logged; felling trees, cutting out the limbs, hauling the logs to the river banks, and piling them up in what they called "landings." When the thaw came and the ice broke up, they got ready to drive to the mills. First, they built a "wanigan," which was simply a floating cook house and headquarters. This was sometimes built by constructing a huge flat-boat, flooring it with rough planks, and building a cook house on it. The more general custom was to tie a large number of logs together into a huge raft, and build a rough shelter on it. In this hut was the stove for the cook, his bunk, spare clothes and tools, and all the supplies needed to last them for the drive.

When they started moving, they never dared to stop. The logs sped along on the crest of the racing flood, and the men rode the logs or ran along the banks with pike pole and cant-hook, preventing a pileup that might result in a dreaded jam. The main idea was to keep the stragglers moving. An advance crew went on ahead to guard the danger spots and to keep the logs in the current.

When night came the wanigan was poled in to the bank and securely tied. The cook prepared the evening meal, constructed a pole table on the bank for the boys to stand by and eat, and built up a huge bonfire. When the tired men came in for supper they were wet to the waist and often to the neck, as they worked in the freezing water. After they ate they sat around the bonfire and dried their clothes, then slept on the ground or in a big tent if the weather was too bad or the rain was too heavy. They were a hardy breed who thus drove the rivers, and they had only contempt for those who were soft and weak.

They were viciously exploited. The robber barons, who stole the timber the lumberjacks so ruthlessly reaped, cared less for their men than they did for the mules and oxen which cost them money. Jacks could be had for the asking. There was no compensation for a sick or injured man, and no insurance to bother about if he was killed. When a camp foreman wanted a crew or replacements, he placed an order with an employment agent, who gathered the required number of men. These recruits signed a slip which deducted two dollars from their first pay, and which was the agent's fee. They were given a ticket to the camp where they were employed, and this also was charged to their account. Blind with drink, they were loaded like cattle into cars on a company owned railroad, and when the train reached the nearest station to the camp they were kicked off, if able to navigate, and thrown out like sacks of grain if they were unconscious with alcohol; as most of them were. Free whiskey was provided for the ride in many cases, to insure their arrival at their destination.

Tossed out into a snow bank at thirty below zero, with his knapsack thrown after him, the drunken wretch was on his own. The train crew didn't care if he froze or survived. It was none of their business. It was a common sight at one of these landings to see half-sober men beating and kicking their sodden companions into motion, to keep them from perishing in the cold. Quite often one man would flail and beat his friend with a knapsack until he got him on his feet, then lead him off on the trail to camp.

Many of the foremen were in "cahoots" with the employment agents, splitting the fee. As soon as a man had worked out what he owed for the job and his train fare, the foreman would fire him and put in a call for more men. As this meant a dollar a head to an unscrupulous foreman, many camps had what they called "the three-crew custom." One crew was working, one was going back to town, and the other was coming to take the place of the one that was temporarily employed! The return to town was often a bitter trip. With no money to pay train fare, it was a case of hike and starve on the way, and this practice continued until the state put a halt to it by law.

The only break these men had was in the nature, size and quality of the meals they ate. Their tables were loaded with stews, roast, and steaks, with fish on Friday in case there should be any conscientious Catholics in camp. They had an abundance of potatoes and other vegetables. Pie was served every day of the year. Huge pancakes were the custom six mornings a week an average of a hundred pancakes every four minutes leaving the top of the stove for the short trip to the tables and the shorter trip down the "Little Red Lane." Cakes, cookies, and jelly were common, served with coffee or tea that would eat the plating off the spoons. The vigorous life and the rugged work enabled the jacks to burn up huge amounts of calories, and indigestion was an unknown word.

When a man got too old to work, he was turned out and cast aside like a broken tool that was too cheap to repair. The few times when an operator was criticised for this heartless practice brought the callous reply, "I didn't make him old. Why blame me?" But the operators *did* make men old before their time, and ruthlessly drained their lives away to fatten their profits and enlarge their bank accounts.

When a jack was in town he turned to flop houses or cheap hotels operated chiefly for loggers, where he could get a room for the average price of 35¢ a night. In Duluth a Gospel Center called "The Bethel" was opened about 1912, where broken and busted men could find shelter. There the boys were fed in a huge dining room freely and without price, and there were three floors of dormitories where a man could get a cot for 15¢ a night. It was a very common sight, when the cots were all full, to see up to a hundred and fifty men sleeping on the floors, seeking shelter from the storms and the bitter cold. The whiskey peddlers took all their money, but left it to better men to provide for their needs when they were broke, friendless, and without hope or help.

More than any other class that ever lived in our land, the old-time lumberjack could truthfully say, "No man cared for my soul." His rough and rude ways would scare the average preacher into hiding. His language would shock a pirate, and his roaring habits when he came to town drove the godly to cover. But better days were to dawn for him, and a strange and new type of Gospel minister was on his horizon when the century closed. Through the efforts of this new company conditions were destined to change, and the comparative luxury of a logger's camp life today can be traced back to the aroused conscience of the State when these Sky Pilots went into action. It is of them that this book now speaks. It is their saga we desire to sing. *They* are the giants who did such great things for God. In these pages you will now meet a few of them.

The city of Duluth was the center out of which the new light was to flow. Its streets roared with woodsmen. It had a wild section known as "The Bowery" which was as tough as the infamous Barbary Coast. It was the most lurid spot in the North at times, and one of the most attractive at others. The name of Duluth is synonymous with romance and revival, and it was the mecca of men who sought the golden fleece. It was fitting that it should also become a fountain of grace and the dawning place of a new era.

# The Sky Pilot

# CHAPTER III

# The Sky Pilot

It was to this fabulous city of Duluth that a lad named Frank Higgins came, seeking an opportunity to secure an education. He had left his Canadian home at Shelburn, Ontario, expecting to return when he had finished his schooling, but his destiny lay elsewhere. He returned at the age of forty-nine years, to die where he had been born. The formal education he sought eluded him, but he blazed new trails of the Spirit and founded an empire for God. He pioneered a new field of evangelism and taught the Christian world a new concept of Home Missions, reaching a sector of humanity for which no spiritual work had ever been done before. The love of the great North was developed in him there in Duluth and its environs, but the consuming passion for Christ he brought with him. And with it he also brought a heart as big as all outdoors, a love for men that burned like a flame, and a desperate desire to see men saved.

Frank Higgins was a huge man, and one of the most powerful physical specimens the North ever saw. He was five feet, eight inches tall, and weighed 236 pounds; every ounce of which seemed bone and muscle. Mel Trotter once described him in these words, "He was an ax-handle and a half across the shoulders, and two ax-handles across the hips." He had a great, booming voice, and a contagious laugh that could set any crowd of jacks chuckling within minutes of his arrival. But his warm and tender heart also caused his cheeks to be wet with tears, as he pleaded with some hardened sinner to take Christ and be born again, or as he wept over the wreck of some life demolished by liquor and its attendant train of sins. The only enemies he ever had were the whiskey peddlers, gamblers, and thieves who resented the inroads on their incomes which Frank's work made – for men who are saved, and are living a Christian life, are no source of profit to the underworld. When he arrived in Duluth, of course, all of this was ahead of him, and he had no idea of what his career was to be. He wanted to enter the ministry and preach the Gospel, but his plans were directed toward a formal pastorate. In his boyhood days in Canada this resolution was formed, and from it he never wavered. He often went out into the woods and preached to the trees and the cattle, using a stump for a pulpit. Whenever he could get a group of his schoolmates to stop and listen, he would practice on them, but if there was no one to hear he just practiced preaching anyhow!

A story, never before told in print, shows Frank's unflagging ardor to proclaim the Gospel. When he had been the Sky Pilot for a few years and fame had already come to him in some part, he was in Duluth on a visit. He was in company with a friend named Charles Goodell, who at that time was a business man of some consequence, acting as the Western Agent for the Austin-Weston Road Grader Company. As the two men strolled down Superior Street, at Fifth Avenue West a third man accosted them and spoke to Mr. Goodell. After a few words together, Mr. Goodell said to his friend, "Gus, I'd like you to meet Frank Higgins."

As they shook hands, Gus said, "This is not *the* Frank Higgins, the Sky Pilot, is it?"

Frank smiled and admitted his identity, whereupon Gus said, "Mr. Higgins, I have wanted to meet you ever since I first heard of your great work. I have also wished I could hear you preach. Indeed, I'd go any distance to hear a sermon from you!"

Frank asked, "Do you mean that?"

Gus answered, "You bet I do!"

"Alright," Frank said, "take off your hat, you are in church!" He stepped off the curb, turned to face the sidewalk, took his pocket Bible out and read a text to his audience of two men. Then in his great voice he started to preach. Three men passing by stopped to listen, five more joined them, and in a few minutes scores of men were crowded around listening to the message of the Cross. For years after that Mr. Goodell was fond of telling the episode, and Gus *never* forgot it! He found Christ in that sermon.

When Frank first arrived in Duluth, an uncouth lad from a small provincial town, he had very little capital and no plans except the determination to get through high school. He was most fortunate in getting a room in the home of a grand woman who was an ardent Methodist, and who encouraged the lad in his desire to enter the ministry. The boy worked at every honest part-time job he could get, and in the summer made his best financial gains by peddling soap from door to door! With axe and saw he was adept, and earned many a dollar cutting firewood. So the years fled by and Frank neared his goal of a high-school diploma which, however, was never to be reached. Before he had earned enough credits for graduation, he had been thrust out into the work of salvaging men, and never achieved his educational aspiration.

Not yet ready for college, and seeing no immediate chance of obtaining a college or seminary degree, Frank came under the care of the Presbytery of Duluth at this time as a student-candidate for future ordination. While pursuing his studies under Presbytery's direction, he was sent to New Duluth as a temporary supply for the then vacant pulpit, and stayed there a year and a half. The congregation would have kept him there for the span of his life, if they could have done so, but a much larger charge at Barnum became vacant, and Frank was sent there to supply for a few weeks until a pastor could be secured.

He stayed three years!

This was the pivot of his life, and the dawning of his great destiny, although he did not know it then. The congregation at Barnum had a number of lumber barons on the roll, and one of the most prominent and most kindly was Martin Cain. He had a real interest in the welfare of his men, and did all he could to safeguard them in the woods and to make their lives comfortable. At that time he was operating on Willow River. One Monday he invited Frank to take a trip up in the woods with him. The young preacher accepted eagerly, because he liked Martin Cain and was always happy when he could spend time in the big timber.

At one of the Willow River Camps, the men were eating an outdoor lunch when Frank and Mr. Cain arrived. After a few minutes conversation with his foreman, Mr. Cain turned to the crowd and said, "Boys, this huge fellow is Frank Higgins. He is our pastor at the church in Barnum. When you are in town some Sunday come and hear him."

The jacks looked Higgins over, admired the width of his shoulders, and one of them said, "A preacher, huh? All right, preacher, give us a sermon."

Frank was somewhat taken aback and said, "I'm sorry, boys, but I have no Bible and no notes with me."

Quite seriously the jack said, "It's a sorry preacher who doesn't have at least ONE sermon in his heart!"

Frank nodded in agreement and said, "Lad, you're right." He climbed up on a stump, recalled as best he could the sermon of the preceding day, and gave them the best that was in him. The men listened with rapt attention while Frank told them about "The Friend of Sinners." Before he was half way through the men were so quiet they seemed almost to have stopped breathing. When the sermon ended, Frank bowed his head and prayed for each man, for his home and family, and for his final salvation. His prayer left them all in tears, and one by one they came up to shake his hand and thank him for his words.

That was the first of many trips with Martin Cain, and

42

his voice was a familiar sound in the camps. Whenever he appeared the men dropped their work and crowded about him, and he dealt with them so tenderly and wisely that many of them turned to Christ and a better way of life.

One night as they sat in camp, the jacks were drying their clothes around the great stove, and Frank was talking to them in an informal way about the consequences of sin and the way of escape. One of the jacks said, "Preacher, what is your greatest ambition in life?" Frank answered, "To pilot men to the skies!" The jack said in all seriousness, "Well, you ought to make a good 'sky pilot;' you seem to know the way." The name stuck, and before many years the whole Christian world knew about the Sky Pilot of the north woods.

In that same conversation one of the other boys said, "What is the matter with preachers, anyhow? Anybody else who has something to sell goes out and peddles it. Preachers wait for someone to come and get it. In these woods there are thirty thousand men, and I'll bet not more than thirty of them hear a sermon a year on the average."

Frank held his breath with amazement and asked, "How many men did you say work in the woods?"

"Thirty thousand."

"And they never hear the Gospel?"

"No sir, they do not. How can they?"

"Well, they're *going* to, brother," Frank concluded, "even if I have to tell it to every one of them myself."

So the great idea was born, and an epic of evangelism began. Frank went back to Barnum and talked with Martin Cain and his fellows, and they enthusiastically encouraged him. He carried the idea to Presbytery and cold water was dashed on the suggestion. He was told that the National Missions Board would have to handle such a project, and they would have to initiate the work. So Frank went after the Board of National Missions, and got exactly nowhere. Nobody had ever preached to lumberjacks before. There was no precedent, there were no funds available, and there were

43

no men trained for that sort of work even if they did have money.

Frank might have been daunted by the obstacles piled in his path, had it not been for a sad episode which occurred just at that time. A lumberjack was brought to the Barnum hospital in the final stages of pneumonia, and the doctor told him it was too late to save him, and that he had only a few hours to live. He asked the doctor to try to get Frank Higgins to pray with him, and the preacher, fortunately, was available.

Frank came into the room, knelt by the sick man's bed, and asked him plainly and simply if he was a Christian. The jack said he was not, so Frank unfolded to him the Way of Life. The fellow accepted Christ as his Saviour, and wistfully said to Frank, "You and Jesus are the only friends I have, I guess. Will you stay with me?"

Frank promised, and the man relapsed into a coma shortly afterward. In about an hour he seemed to rally. He turned his eyes to the preacher and said, "If it had not been for you I would have died lost. Promise me you will go back to the camps and tell the boys about the Jesus you showed me!" Frank pressed the dying man's hand and gave his promise. He walked out of there a few moments later bound by that promise, and spent the rest of the years of his life making good on that pledge. Realizing that he would get no help from the ecclesiastic authorities and that he was on his own, he began to look for ways and means of evangelizing the men in the woods. He neglected his pastoral work and his studies preaching on Sundays in his pulpit, and spending the rest of the week in the camps. In this he was abetted and encouraged by Martin Cain and the elders of the Barnum Church, who were in complete sympathy with their preacher's ambition to make salvation available to the lost legion of the timber lands. Many long and hard miles the evangelist hiked through the woods, the love of Christ driving him and the love of men making the miles easy and his pack light. So passed the spring and summer, and Frank Higgins made the grace of God known wherever Martin Cain had a camp.

Early in the fall, Frank learned that the church at Bemidji was without a pastor. This was just what he wanted, as it was well up toward the northern border, and right in the midst of the larger lumber camps. He prevailed upon Presbytery to install him there as supply, and took up his great adventure. He followed the pattern he had set at Barnum, preaching in his pulpit on Sunday, and spending all the rest of the week in the camps. At first he was greeted with amazement and some suspicion, as the men could not believe that any person had an unselfish purpose in seeking them and sharing their dangers and discomfort. Altruism was a quality a lumberjack rarely met, if ever. But as the weeks passed, and the men learned to admire and respect the short giant who entered into their work, their sports, their sorrows, and their troubles, the way became easy. His visits were eagerly awaited, and when his stocky form appeared trudging down a tote-road with his knapsack on his back, the whole camp welcomed him. In his knapsack he carried a few necessities and a great load of Bibles, song books, reading material and small comforts for the men. Many a stout fellow "hefted" that pack and marvelled that any man could carry it mile after mile. Indeed, it was the great weight of that heavy "turkey" which finally caused the Sky Pilot's death.

On him rested the mantle of God! His words were words of grace and love. His messages burned with the fires of faith, and his prayers melted the hearts of his hearers. Certain of his biographers have sought to glamourize Frank Higgins by over-emphasizing his tremendous strength and fighting ability, but those who knew him best remember him for his warm heart, his unchanging love for the rough, rude, lusty and lustful crowd he called "my boys," and for the fact that he lived to make Jesus known to lost sinners. Most of these apocryphal stories have some basis of fact, of course, as his life was adventurous and robust. He *did* plunge into a saloon when necessary, and carry out one of the boys who had fallen into the hands of harpies, and woe to the person who got in his way or tried to prevent the rescue! But for every such episode there were a thousand occasions when his tender spirit was shown in deeds of kindness and mercy, as he quietly and calmly shouldered some other man's burden.

As an instance of how such stories grow in the telling, let me recite one which I have heard scores of times, which is usually told as being typical of Frank's methods of procedure. At one camp, the narrator states, Frank was having a Sunday afternoon service and a man was heckling him. After vainly trying to shut the fellow up by appealing to his better nature, Frank hauled off and struck the disturber a mighty blow. The force of the punch lifted the heckler off his feet, turned him over in the air, and left him headfirst in a rain barrel! While his friends pulled him out, Frank calmly proceeded to finish his sermon!

Now let me retell the story as it *really* occurred, and as I got it from Elwyn Channer. There is no man living who knew Frank better, nor who loved him more dearly. Remember that lumberjacks are a playful gang, and that they are always pulling, scuffling, wrestling, and shoving like small boys on a school ground. And Frank was right in the midst of any frolic which was started at any time.

Near the door of each camp it was customary to set a huge barrel and fill it with water. There it was handy in case of fire, and the men used it to fill their wash basins on the rare occasions when they washed or shaved. They also used the water barrel when they washed their clothes, and did not want to go all the way to the stream. One afternoon Frank was talking to a group of jacks, and a scuffle began. As the gleeful contenders surged past him, one of them made the mistake of picking on Frank. With a joyful bellow the Sky Pilot swung his huge arm to grab the jack, who tried to duck away. Frank's forearm hit the luckless chap in the chest with such force it lifted him off the ground and deposited him *sitting* in the water barrel, where he, the victim, led the howls of laughter at his own plight.

But Frank rarely if ever had to fight for the right to preach. He had a hundred men in every camp who would gladly do that for him whenever trouble started! But his own kindly and genial nature, coupled with his natural and unfeigned love for men, would preclude the idea that he could be the rough bruiser which some writers have portrayed him.

The church at Bemidji proved an ideal base for the camp work, and weeks went by during which the town saw the pastor only on Sundays. The woods claimed six-sevenths of his time. When winter settled down, the Sky Pilot put on snowshoes and continued his rounds. When the snow packed he changed to skis, and dragged a toboggan behind him, on which he transported his familiar load of Bibles, hymnals, and literature. Then one day a man, desperately sick, had to be taken from a camp to the hospital, and Frank dragged him on the toboggan over the crusted snows. The trip was so hard and the toil so bitter, the Sky Pilot realized he had to have some means of transportation, and set his nimble mind to solve this problem. He hit upon the idea of training a dog team, and out of Bemidji in a short time he operated the first dog-drawn ambulance the woodsmen had ever seen or heard of.

With this aid the preacher could increase his weight of supplies, so he was able to stay out longer and travel farther from his base. When the spring came he retired his dogs to a well-earned rest. Many a sick or injured jack had ridden "outside" to a hospital and adequate medical aid behind those missionary dogs, and many an expectant mother had made the same trip in safety and comfort. Doing enough work to kill two ordinary men, the Little Giant thrived and rejoiced in his original ministry, and his name became a legend among the lumberjacks. Whenever he went into a strange camp or into new territory, he needed only to announce his name, and respectful attention was accorded him by the roughest elements humanity knows. The sheer manhood and virility of the preacher were his passport among the strong men, and his loving heart was the key which unlocked every door he wished to enter.

So passed the months, until the week Frank was so deep in the woods he could not get home for his Sunday services. This did not worry him, as he knew that the session of the church had elders in its ranks who could preach or handle the service, so he stayed and finished out the Sunday preaching to the jacks. When he returned the following Tuesday, he arrived just in time to attend the regular session meeting of the church. When the meeting had been properly constituted with prayer, and before any business was transacted, the senior elder very gravely asked the pastor where he had been on Sunday.

Frank replied, "I was stuck out in the woods. I could not get back, so I stayed and preached to the men in the camp. I knew you men could care for the meeting here. By the way, who led the service?"

After some silence the senior elder said, "We did not *have* any service. We waited a long time for our pastor, and when he did not appear we dismissed the crowd and went home. Now, Frank, this has to stop. You have been neglecting the parish for the woods ever since you have been here. You have to choose between being pastor of this church and being an evangelist to the lumberjacks, but you can't be both. We don't mean to press you. Take all the time you want to reach a decision."

Promptly the preacher replied, "I don't *need* any time, and I *have* made a decision! This pulpit is vacant right now! A thousand men could take this church. The boys in the woods have only me. Furthermore, I am disgusted with you and ashamed of the fact that all of you men together could not conduct the church in an emergency for one Sunday! You are supposed to be ordained elders, and not one of you could or would act in my absence. I wouldn't be pastor of a bunch like you for any money. Pick another man!"

The next day he was back in the woods on the ceaseless round of mercy and evangelism to which he was peculiarly ordained of God. With no salary to depend on, and no house to live in, Frank's wife, whom he had married at Barnum, took their baby daughter and went to live on a farm which she owned at Delano. From then on Frank called that "home" and made it the base of his operations. By the very nature of his work his home-life was broken and spasmodic, and he was almost a stranger to his own family. Driven by his passion for souls he sacrificed every personal interest and laboured for God and "his boys." In the bleak winters, when it was forty below and colder, he travelled by snowshoes, skis, and dog sled. In the summer he went on foot or by canoe, as the circumstances and territory decided.

All of this time he was still under care of Presbytery as a candidate for the ministry, and year by year he came seeking ordination, but each time he was frustrated by his lack of formal education. He appealed to the Board of National Missions for aid in his camp work, but there was no money alloted for evangelizing lost lumberjacks. Martin Cain had his hand in his pocket most of the time. Luke Marvin and other godly elders of the First Presbyterian Church in Duluth came to his aid with financial help, and friends all over the country contributed as they heard of the great work he was doing.

Such a light could not long be concealed beneath the proverbial bushel, and within a few years the fame of the Sky Pilot spread widely, and his name was well-known. Then some of his friends decided to capitalize on his reputation and popular appeal, and make one more effort to ordain him. By that time Frank did not care whether they succeeded or not, as the mantle of God's peace and power very evidently clothed him. But he appeared before Presbytery, and when Frank's friends presented the case for his ordination, it was unanimously agreed that he had earned the honour and dignity, and without further delay the Presbytery of Duluth ordained Frank Higgins as evangelist to all of the lumberjacks in the United States. And in so doing they honoured *themselves* more than they did this great hero of the Cross.

Now help came to him. Obviously no one man could adequately cover a parish that was two hundred miles square, and populated by thirty thousand men. Especially when most of the travelling had to be done on foot or by canoe, in rain, snow, ice, and sleet, and in temperatures which varied between 90 degrees above zero to 50 degrees below. To his aid he called other giants of the spirit, each of them a stalwart in his own right. Some of these assistant pilots were men who had found Christ through Frank's efforts, and any and all of them were devoted to his interests. He had the native ability to bind men to him in loyalty and affection, as his own sweet spirit stirred a response in those who became acquainted with him. The jacks called all of these men "sky pilots," and when they had been a month in the camps it would have been hard to have told the preacher from the crew! They shared the lives and hardships of the men of their wild parish, and did heroic service for God.

Among these early colleagues were such men as Fred Davis, Jack McCall, Matt Daly, Pete Peterson, John McGinnis, Dick Farrell, and Al Channer. The latter two are the sole survivors of this gallant company who, like the famed "Light Brigade" counted their lives as naught, ignored the odds against them, and battled for God against sin and Satan. Dick Farrell, like John Sornberger, was an ex-pugilist and every one of this group was capable of giving a good account of himself in a brawl. But they avoided trouble when they could. Their purpose was to preach Christ, not to win fights– although none of them ever ran from trouble of any sort. Out of this group Frank formed the famed "Shanty Men's Association," and under this name the company went forth to spread the dragnet of the Gospel over the north woods.

The burden of finance fell largely upon Frank. His men worked for a bare living, fifty dollars a month being the average "salary" (?) paid each of the workers. When the treasury warranted the strain, each man was also allowed five dollars a month for travelling expenses! Frank travelled from church to church, spoke to clubs and groups, solicited his personal friends, and used every legitimate means to keep the work financed and managed to make ends meet by the end of each month. On one occasion he even put a mortgage on his wife's farm at Delano to pay his workers and keep the mission alive.

So passed the early years before the break came. The report of his activities had spread and aroused great interest, and Frank was invited to attend the General Assembly of the Presbyterian Church and speak about his field and labours. His simple, forceful personality captured the commissioners, and he was an immediate sensation. The Board of National Missions finally woke up to what was going on and Frank was offered a position under the Board. He was made the official missionary of the Board to the lumberjacks, given a free hand to plan and execute his own program, and to choose his own helpers. This relieved him from the heavy burden of raising the money, put the work on a stable basis, and it looked as though his troubles were over.

But scarcely six months passed before an almost fatal blow was struck against the plan. A minister of the co-called "liberal" school, jealous of the popularity of the Sky Pilot and highly antagonistic to the Gospel as these men preached it, brought serious charges against Frank before the Board. The Sky Pilot immediately went to New York, resigned his commission, and stated his demands for a full and complete investigation of the charges. Six months dragged by, during which Frank was again limited to his own resources. But he never faltered in his stride nor missed a day in the woods, preaching as he had been doing for years.

All of his crew stayed by him, and the jacks were furious

at the slander. If Frank had consented they would have ended the affair in a matter of hours. Their suggested remedies went all the way from tar and feathers to a rope and a limb for the man who had slandered their champion. But Frank laughed off all of their extreme suggestions, and a commission made an exhaustive inquiry into the charges. Their report cleared Frank completely, convicted the accuser of slander, calumny, and false witness against a brother minister, and the wretch was deposed from the ministry. When Frank received the telegram reinstating him as the representative of the Board, he just thanked God, rolled his sleeves a little higher, and went right on in the way he had been going. "There were giants in the earth in those days" in truth. The life of any one of these men would make an epic which only Kipling or Richard Harding Davis could properly write, and Frank Higgins was the greatest of them all. The mantle of God never rested upon a greater man than he, and his name is still a legend in the woods. With all of his work of administration and supervision, he still found time to conduct upwards of three hundred services a year in the camps. When the lumber and cedar camps were not open, he went up and down the river and among the railroad crews. Men were his material and he sought them wherever they were. He took the church to the congregation!

His passion for souls never faltered. Al Channer once told me of the last conference Frank ever had with his staff of camp-evangelists. He was on his way to Chicago to submit to his third and last operation; the one which ended his life. It was a last and desperate chance that was offered him by surgery and, characteristically, he took it. He called a meeting of his men in the Duluth Y. M. C. A., and to this final historic meeting came Daly, Davis, McCall, Sornberger, and Channer.

Frank stood before them and told them of his one chance for recovery, and said he was on his way to the hospital. Then he reviewed the work they had done together, and laid it on their hearts to continue. With tears rolling down his cheeks, the leader finished by saying, "Oh for the days when I could go back into the woods, take the boys by the hand and call them by name: Jim, and John, and Bill. I wish I could turn back the curtain of time and do it all over again. But that I cannot do, and if I have come to the end of the trail *you* will have to do it for me." And he sent those faithful men forth to carry on the Gospel ministry he had begun. To their eternal credit, every one of them died in the harness, except Channer and Farrell, who still live and labour among the men of the woods. Dick Farrell is in the camps of Idaho and Channer travels the woods of Minnesota–the last of the giants!

But many, fruitful, happy years were to pass before Higgins fell in the fray, and the forces of darkness came to fear his power and influence. He had but one theme: "Christ died for our sins," and his favourite text was, "Jesus, the Friend of Sinners." He radiated the presence of Christ wherever he went, and the love of the Lord was engendered in the hearts of some of the roughest men our civilization ever knew. That statement is not derogatory of the men. They were the product of their environment. Living in the deep woods where no culture or pleasure could reach them, fighting heat and cold, fire and flood, battling nature in her wildest moods and fighting each other for a pastime, the old-time jack was a hard-cast citizen. His only contact with women was generally with the wrong sort, his club was a whisky peddler's den, and he was separated from his family about eight months a year. He deserved sympathy more than censure, and from Higgins he got it! The Sky Pilot was a *gentle* giant, ordained of God to originate the most unique ministry any man ever experienced.

No record was ever compiled of the results of his twenty years in the woods, nor could such a total be estimated. The men were nomads, footloose wanderers. They drifted from job to job and camp to camp. But they carried the Gospel with them as they went, and their lives were different after they found Christ. One night when Al Channer was preaching in a large city mission, a man came up after the service to shake hands. He said, "Twenty years ago I was converted in a meeting in a camp, and I have never seen you since. I can still give you the text upon which you preached that night!" There were multiplied hundreds of such men whose experience was identical. Of those who remained on the job Bible classes were formed, and in the course of time they were able to argue intelligently for the Christian premise, and they became personal workers and a stabilizing influence in the camps. The present day logger is a gentleman compared to the jacks of the past generation, and his mode of living is reasonably comfortable. The great improvement can be credited in a large part to the Sky Pilots, who adventured for God and brought changed conditions by the force of their Gospel and the impact of their personalities.

Broken men were repaired and given a new lease on life. Drunkards were turned into sober citizens. Families were reunited and crimes expiated in the wake of the Sky Pilot as the years piled up, and the work gathered momentum. Then a cloud appeared on the horizon, and Frank learned that even giants are human. For two decades he had battled storm and cold, carrying seventy-five pounds in his pack, and the irritation of the pack-straps across his shoulders finally produced a spot so sore he realized he must have medical attention. The surgeon diagnosed the case as sarcoma, brought on by the constant weight of the pack. He advised an immediate operation, as the case was far advanced, and he held out small hope of a complete recovery. Frank decided at once to submit to the operation, and the surgeon did his best for the famed evangelist.

The patient was very slow to rally, and the doctors, greatly concerned, decided upon a series of blood transfusions. A call went out, and in a few hours a delegation of eight rough men appeared at the hospital. They stated that they were lumberjacks who had come to give their blood for the man who had given his life to them. The leader said, "If there ain't blood enough in us eight men, say the word and every man in Northern Minnesota will be on his way down here tomorrow!"

Another delegate said, "Doc, if Frank Higgins needs blood, meat, or bones, I'll get a thousand men here in twenty-four hours for you to whittle on!" And he meant it. He spoke the sober and restrained truth.

The Sky Pilot made a slow recovery, and after a number of weeks they told him, "Your days are numbered, and the number is small. If you have affairs you wish to take care of you had better be about it."

Frank went back to Shelburn, and there in the peace and quiet of his native Canadian home he slowly regained a measure of strength and fooled his physician by making a partial recovery. He went back to his labours, preaching under the desperate drive of the conscious knowledge that his days were numbered. Not one waking minute was free from pain, and the hours of the night dragged by as agony of body drove sleep from his pillow. But no word of complaint ever came from his lips, and his courageous heart would not admit defeat. For six long, pain-filled years he toured the country, tramped and rode the woods, and preached to men who knew he was dying on his feet. Perhaps the very handicap under which he laboured worked to the advantage of his ministry, as the men of the woods gave the more earnest heed to the words of a man almost dead. They were fruitful years, and live in the memory of those who knew him.

He was a giant to the end, although a weak and trembling giant. The spirit of the man burned the brighter as the days grew shorter, and twice more surgeons tried to save his life by the application of their utmost skill. But the third operation ended his battle, and the giant fell. He returned to his home in Shelburn for a final rest, and there he fell on sleep, his labours done.

He had a great entering into life eternal!

The Board of National Missions sent a representative to Canada to bring his body back for burial, and he sleeps today

Some of Frank Higgins' Boys

An Old Time Logging Crew

A Typical Logging Camp

Camp 29, Headquarters of International Lumber Company

at Delano, in the heart of the country he evangelized for Christ.

Four of his colleagues attended the final rites, together with a great host of ministers and laymen, who came to do honour to a fallen hero. Chief among them was a delegation of unshaven men, dressed in calked boots and stagged pants, with the callouses of ax-handle, cant-hook, and peavey on their palms. They shed few tears and they spoke no words, but the jacks were the real and sincere mourners at the funeral of Frank Higgins, the original Sky Pilot.

Frank Higgins built no churches and established no fixed organizations for worship, his monument was made of flesh and blood, and was built from the redeemed lives of thousands. Such men need no marble shafts to commemorate their names. They live in the hearts of those they served.

So the mantle was empty, and its occupant could use it no more. But the work of God does not cease when a worker goes to his great and well-earned reward, and the mantle fluttered about seeking new shoulders whereon to rest. It did not long delay its choice, for God never ends one man's career in His service until He has his successor prepared. The man destined to wear the mantle of the apostolic succession in the diocese of the North Woods was at the funeral and of him we shall now read.

# BOOK TWO

## The Bull of the Woods

# Adventure's Darling

# CHAPTER I

# Adventure's Darling

When John Whitman Sornberger opened his eyes to the light of day, none of his family dreamed that this new baby was to be adventure's darling, destined to become far too familiar with the bright face of danger. Indeed, when the law officers of four states were searching for him a little more than a score of years later, his father stated with anguish of spirit and sadness of heart, "If I'd known how he was going to turn out, I'd have strangled him in his cradle the day he was born, and saved us all a heap of heartbreak!" But on that twenty-seventh day of July in the year 1869, to his father he was but one more mouth to feed; to his mother, just another baby to love. Although hard money was a rare thing in the affairs of the family, the elder Sornberger was an industrious, capable, hard-working man, and there was always plenty for all. Both he and his wife were devout Christians, and no child ever had a better background or more reason to succeed in life. Every factor that produces decent citizenship was available for the making of this baby. He had a Christian home, where the dignity of labour imparted that sense of independence and self-reliance which makes a man proud of his accomplishments.

When John was seven years old his dear mother died, and the home in Montreal was broken up. His father moved to Northern Minnesota, where he took up a homestead and timber claim, and worked in the woods to earn money to develop his farm. He was a hale and hearty man, and when he died at the age of 93 he had completed seventy-four years as a lumberman. Undoubtedly, it was from him that John inherited his tremendous strength and rugged constitution; that strength which first led him into the paths of crime and caused him to become outlawed, and *then* was used of God to such effect and purpose as to make him one of the greatest of the Apostles of the Pines.

What his life might have been if his mother had lived no one can say, but at her death the lad went to live with an uncle in Niagara Falls, where he was welcomed, loved, and made a member of the family. This brother of John's father was a wonderful man, a great Christian who was noted for his knowledge of the Word and his ability as a teacher, and who lived his preachments in his own daily affairs. Once again it is interesting to speculate as to the course of the boy's later life if he could have stayed with this grand person, his uncle, but his lot was not so to be. At the age of eleven he left his uncle's house, which had been a true home to him, and went to Minnesota to join his dad. Since Mr. Sornberger was working in the woods at the time, and could not take an eleven year old lad into that rough and vile environment, a home for the boy was found with a family that agreed to take him in as a boarder.

Already grown to a husky size which was prophetic of his future strength, the boy so endeared himself to the people with whom he found shelter that they made repeated efforts to adopt him as their own son. And again the fancy likes to dwell on "what might have been"—for these folks also were sincere and devout in the practice of the Christian faith. But John's father was reluctant to give up his son, and when he consulted his brother-in-law, the Hon. W. H. Campbell, a man well known in the politics of his day, this uncle also refused to permit the adoption. Certainly no lad ever had a better chance to get the proper start in life, and at first it seemed as though John was on the right road.

He stayed in this foster home until he had finished the

sixth grade, which was destined to be the end of his formal schooling, although not of his education. He was learning until the day of his death. Since the boys of almost any region are smaller editions of the men of that time and place, it was inevitable that the lads on the fringe of the frontier should pattern their conduct after the rough and rude men who made up their masculine world. Each town and village had its youthful bully, and every new-comer had to fight for the right to live in any semblance of peace. The sports were all virile, and in place of baseball, basketball and football, the practice of hunting, fishing, fighting, and what was colloquially called, "Hell-raising in general" lightened the leisure hours, such as there were. When young John entered the Pine Rapids School, almost 12 years of age, he was nearly as large as any fourteen year old boy in the group. The local lads spent the major part of the first day sizing up the new lad, whom they dubbed, "That Canuck." As soon as the school ended and the boys started home, John was halted at the edge of the clearing by the youthful mob. He was neither surprised nor alarmed. He knew the customs and the code, and was not only resigned to the inevitable but was joyfully anticipating it. The leader of the local lads planted himself before John and said, "If you're gonna live around here you gotta fight er git yer pants kicked off!" Then he pointed to the three largest boys in the crowd and said, "You kin have yer pick. Which of them do you wanta fight?"

John, quiet and unassuming, had already sized up every possible opponent. He had not been idle all day, and had a pretty shrewd idea of the fighting potentials of every boy big enough to concern him, and he had already identified the official bully of the school grounds.

Pointing his finger at the bully, John quietly said, "I'll fight him first." Then turning to the other two in order, he continued, "And when I get him licked, that I'll take that feller and then him on the end last." This, incidentally, was

63

his unvarying custom until he died: tackle the hardest task *first*, and clean up the rest in the order of their challenge and difficulty.

The local gang could hardly believe its ears. But when they convinced themselves that the new lad was serious, a howl of derision went up to the sky. But John went quietly about his preparations. First, he piled up a little mound of good-sized rocks, then he laid a stout club on the pile. As he was taking his coat off, one of the gang asked in a voice sharp with suspicion, "What's the idea of the rocks and the club?"

John's face didn't change expression nor did his voice depart form the calm level of casual conversation as he replied, "That's in case more'n *two* of you jump me at the same time."

The boys exchanged dubious looks, and the bully didn't seem as anxious to fight as he had been. He said, "Well, look, kid, maybe we can just let you go this time without no fight."

John had his coat and shirt off by this time, and he stepped in front of his chosen adversary and said, "But I *wanna* fight!" and hit him without further preliminaries. The noted Bob Fitzsimmons had not yet introduced his famous "solar plexus" punch to the sporting world, but luck was with young John, and his first blow, backed by all his stocky strength, landed in that most vulnerable area. The stricken bully gasped and went slack, practically out on his feet. Not knowing that, John hit him again—a sweeping roundhouse right that struck high on his opponent's cheek. He went down like a felled tree, and, true to the ethics of the time and place, John planted a foot in his face and messed it up all over its breadth. He waited a few seconds, and when it became apparent that this fight was ended, John stepped over to the second opponent and said, "All right, you're next."

But this lad was not having any! He hastily backed

away and said, "Not me! I changed my mind. I ain't *gonna* fight you!"

John turned to the third boy and said, "I guess that leaves it up to you and me."

"No, it don't," exclaimed that boy in very decided tones, "I ain't fighting you neither. Anybody what kin lick Sam there in two wallops and put the boots to *him* is too much fighter for *me*. I'm out of it."

John studied the two for a long moment, then said, "All right, I'll fight the two of you, both at once. And if that don't suit you, pick out any other one kid and I'll fight all three of you."

There was no doubt he meant it, and the calm, quiet announcement convinced the gang more than all the bluster and bragging possibly could have done. There was a unanimous rejection of the plan, and John calmly put on his shirt and coat and strode on home without even a backward glance for his fallen enemy. The boys did not know it then, of course, but they had just witnessed the first public display of the pattern of a life that was never to deviate from the principle. To the day he died, John Sornberger fought every issue, every crisis, every opponent in just exactly that fashion. He licked the hardest one first, and then, if necessary took on the whole world that opposed him. Perhaps heredity had something to do with this: his father was Dutch and his mother Scottish, and neither of those races have ever been wanting in dogged courage and tenacity of purpose.

Northern Minnesota in 1880 was a wild and rugged land, and all of the sports and pleasures of a growing boy were such as you would expect to find in a frontier region. Hunting and fishing were a part of normal living. Swimming, boating, ice skating and hockey were the common modes of relaxation, and of these John had his full share. Like all growing boys in that time and place, he had little time for play; work claimed his strength most of the day. He swung an axe and pulled on one end of a two-man cross-cut saw, he cared for the stock and drove teams of oxen or horses as the need arose. With cant-hook, pike pole or peavey he was soon adept, and could ride a log in fast water with the best of them. He discovered quite early in his youth that he possessed that natural cooperation of eye and nerve which goes to make an expert marksman, and practice in his youth gave him that deadly accuracy with firearms which made him so feared when he became an outlaw. I once met an aging law enforcement officer, who passed up a half dozen chances to arrest John when he, the sheriff, was alone. He frankly confessed that he was afraid to touch his gun for fear John would kill him. And since John only once let an officer get behind him, and was clever enough to dodge them when they ganged up on him in a posse, he walked the woods for years when he should have been in jail!

With rifle, pistol, or shot gun, I never saw John Sornberger miss a shot, and this skill was developed in his youth. For six years he lived and thrived in wild Itasca County, where the Mississippi is born. Chippewa Indians taught him to handle a canoe, and when he was 16 he could out-paddle any two Indians in the North woods. He knew the wild Mississippi in its every reach and curve, and the lakes and sloughs which had been the highways for the trappers and fur traders were as familiar to him as the streets of your home city are to you. His father taught him the use of snowshoes, and he was like a swallow when skis were beneath his feet. When he hit the trail his pack out-weighed the pack of any other man in the party, and very often he came into camp at night the freshest of the lot, toting some other man's packsack as well as his own.

So for six years the boy lived and learned, grew and developed and built himself a reputation as a fine worker and an enthusiastic fighter. He hated a bully so intensely he never acted as one, and even the men he whipped in combat became his friends and admirers. An ex-prize fighter, seeking refuge in the woods from the law, took a fancy to John and taught him foot-work and ring craft, but the lad fought only for the love of combat, and laughed with the joy of living as he fought.

When John was 18 years old, he was a man in all senses of the word. His uncle, then in the state legislature, had taken a hand in his training, and John had been reading law and studying under such guidance as the uncle could provide. At the age of 18 he was judged ready by his tutors and he went to St. Cloud to enter law school. He had one other purpose in making the trip; he wanted to find and visit his father, who was then a foreman at a camp of the Gilman Lumber Company near St. Cloud. In his father's absence the lad had been operating the family homestead in the Aitkin woods, the arrangement being quite typical of the frontier, where a boy of 15 years of age was generally counted as a man, with all the responsibility and labour of an adult. At 18 John had his full height, five feet ten inches in his socks, but was slender and lithe, not yet having filled out his frame to the stocky two hundred pounds plus which he later possessed.

Many a famed rough-house battler learned to his sorrow, however, that the boy's slender form concealed the power of a tightly wound steel spring, and his body was as tough as rawhide and as hard as a hickory knot. As his fame spread beyond the Grand Rapids woods, noted bar-room brawlers travelled over a hundred miles to try conclusions with John, who joyfully met all comers on the terms, "no holds barred, no rules apply." He was like a shadow on his feet, and could kick a man in the chin almost as skilfully as he could hit him there with his hands. In many a "friendly" scrap he encouraged a burly, slow opponent to clinch with him, so as to practice a score of crippling holds and tricks which he had learned the hard way. Understand, in all of this there was neither malice nor meanness: it was the natural exuberance of a lusty frontier lad whose wild brawling nature demanded an outlet in physical exertion. He could drink with the best of them, fight with the worst of them, and lend his meager funds to any of them who were in need.

John Sornberger never was a habitual drunkard, although fictionalized reports of him have so declared. When he was flush with money he would go off on a spree until he was broke, and then would not touch a drop of liquor again for months. The short time he was in law school he never touched a drink, and kept out of trouble, bar-rooms, and fights. But his financial stake was meager, and in a few months he had reached the bottom of the barrel. He went up into the woods to visit the Gilman Camp and see his dad, and while there the big boss asked him how he was doing in school. John replied, "I did all right while my money lasted, but I'm busted now and have to hunt a job." The boss grinned and said, "Quit hunting. You've got one. I need a man in the office who can count up to more than ten, and who can read something more than big print. When do you want to go to work?"

John said, "Yesterday!"

The boss laughed and said, "Well, it's the tenth of the month. I'll put you on the payroll starting the first, so you have ten days credit at the store if you need clothes."

This ended his formal education as far as schools were concerned; all of his subsequent study was with the aid of tutors and friendly preachers. But it was a long time and a tough road was travelled before John Sornberger ever got interested in "book learning" after he reverted to the woods.

Being young, he naturally drifted with the gang, and was soon adept at every vice which passed for amusement in the camps. For a while his father's influence served as a partial check on his activities, as the old gentleman was a typically Old Testament Christian. He had a stern code of morals and rigid standard of conduct for himself, and could make no allowances for weakness in others. He did not drink, and would as soon have handled live coals as a deck of cards. But shortly after John came into the camp, the elder Sornberger went back to Grand Rapids and John was left with no anchor and no withstanding influence. Then he cut loose and went all out. Having shrewd judgment and Scottish caution, he soon had all of the poker players in camp in debt to him, and got an exalted idea of his ability as a gambler. The winter ended, the crew was paid off, and all went "outside" for a grand spree.

John landed at Delano with his pockets lined with wages and ill-gotten gains, and with a plan to get rich in a hurry. He was going to clean out all of the professional gamblers in Delano, go on to Grand Rapids and do the same, and then retire on his rich winnings. Forty-eight hours after he hit Delano he was busted, without a thin dime in his pockets. He never bucked a professional gambler again! One was enough, and he learned the hard way that "an amateur can't beat a professional at his own game."

John's best friend in Delano owned the largest saloon in town, and the lad went to him and asked for any kind of job he could find for him. The saloon keeper said, "Why, John, come and work for me. I need a bartender who can stay sober and who won't steal more than half of what I take in. This is a break for both of us."

John said, "I never tended bar, how can I mix drinks?" His friend replied, "You won't have to. You can open a bottle and push out a glass, can't you? You have been around here long enough to know we don't mix drinks. *We* mix *drunks*!" So, with a shout of laughter at his own wit, the owner put John on the payroll, and a new phase of life began for him. He had seen liquor from the *front* of the bar, now he got a look at it from the other side. Beneath the bar was parked some standard equipment for a frontier saloon, consisting of a black-jack, for quieting obstreperous customers, a sawed-off shot gun, to discourage hold-ups, and a bottle of knock-out drops, to help part a fool and his money even sooner!

But John thought he really was a man of substance and prestige as he paraded behind the bar, swathed in a long white apron. He practiced saying, "Name yer poison, gents!" until he could roll it out nonchalantly, and practiced even more diligently to palm half of the customer's change without getting caught. The *sober* customers—that is: no bartender in his right mind would ever *think* of offering change to a drunken jack. The boss would only get it in that case, and the law was "every man for himself."

This was strange training for an apostle, but in later years the tricks John learned tending bar stood him in good stead when he started preaching against liquor. He kept many a poor lumber-jack out of an early grave because he knew just how to handle him and sober him up, and it all turned out to good purpose in the end. However, it is not a course of study to be recommended to the average theological seminary!

One day as the budding bartender was resting during a lull, the door swung open and a group of lumbermen came in for a social glass. They were all noted men who controlled vast sections of timber and operated their own mills and camps. One of the richest of them was Mr. C. E. Buckman, who had watched John for some months past and had a great liking for him. In great surprise at the boy's position behind the bar, the lumber king said, "Hullo, Jack! What are you doing *behind* the bar? Helping out a friend?" "No, sir," John replied with considerable pride, "I'm working here now!" Mr. Buckman scowled at him for a long minute and asked, "How did a good lad like *you* ever come down so low as to take up tending bar? You know this is no place for a decent man to be working. What brought it about?"

Suddenly John saw himself in the mirror of this fine

man's mature opinion, and all of the glamour of bartending melted away. He flushed with embarrassment, leaned over the bar and said, "Well, Mr. Buckman, to tell the truth, I was broke. I had to take any job I could get until I can get back in the woods again where I belong."

The operator looked relieved and said, "Well, Jack, you are practically there now. I am in desperate need of a cook in my largest camp near Grand Rapids, and I've eaten enough of your grub to know you can hold down the job. You're hired and your pay starts right now. Go over to the Delano Hotel and get yourself a room while my crew is coming up from the Twin Cities, and we'll all ride out to camp together."

Without a word, John hung up his apron, took out of the till the exact amount he had coming in wages, wrote a note to the saloon owner thanking him for the job, and ended his short career as a bartender. With plenty of flunkies to help, John presided over the cook house and mess hall, and settled down to more honest toil. Unfortunately, the camp was near Grand Rapids, and in that early day about one building in every three in the brawling town was a saloon or tavern. Every pay day John drifted in with the gang, drank up his money, and staggered back for a sobering round of labour. None of the saloons had a lock on the door since they were open day and night. The men came and went in a steady stream 24 hours a day as long as their money lasted—or as long as there was a chance of getting more booze without cash.

John had been living peacefully for almost a year, chiefly because nobody who knew who he was would fight with him. The turn came, however, when he was standing near the end of the bar one night, pockets empty and thirst still unsatisfied. A huge jack walked in who was practically sober, and who was well heeled financially. John took one look at him, saw he was a stranger, and called his cronies into conference. They listened closely to his orders, nodded comprehension, and quietly surrounded the visitor. When John gave the signal, they fell upon him, tripped him flat on the floor, grabbed him by the ankles and hoisted him up feet first. They shook him vigorously until all of his money rolled out. John was watching for it, and grabbed it as fast as it fell. When the jack was picked clean, they dropped him to the floor and lined up to the bar. John slapped the money on the bar and said, "Drinks for the house." Then he turned to the stranger and courteously invited him to join the party and "drink up with the rest of the boys!"

There was nothing new or original in this procedure, it was a common practice in the north woods. A smart man could salvage some of his resources by hurrying to the bar and getting as many drinks as he could down before the cash was gone, and if the victim was a little slow he often arrived at the fount too late to partake of his own hospitality!

This stranger made that tactical error. He shoved through the crowd until he faced John, and exclaimed in wrath, *"You* put them up to that, you skinny little whelp! No pasty-faced kid can put anything over on *me* like that. I'm gonna give you the licking of your life!" He outweighed John 80 pounds and was three inches taller, so he had some justification for his misplaced confidence. Misplaced, because as he was winding up to swing on John, the boy went into action. He was all over his opponent before the man could get set, and in four minutes they were both all over the barroom. The crowd whooped with delight, and between bursts of blasphemy the stranger slugged with all he had. He never had a chance. After the first minute John knew he could take the poor fellow anytime he got ready, and he played him like a fish on the line. Then, beginning to tire, John stepped in close and ended it with a stiff uppercut, which put the big man to sleep for seven minutes. When he came to he was alone with the bartender. He leaned on the bar for support, and the bartender handed him a stiff jolt of Panther Juice and said, "Here, pal! It's on the house. You need it and you earned it."

The stranger tossed off the drink, felt his swollen chin and asked, "Who was that?"

"That," said the bartender with pride in the local product, "was Jack Sornberger!"

The visiting delegate looked at him for a long minute and said, "I'll be back!" Then he turned and went out into the night.

John and his gang had gone back to the camp by the next morning, and the stranger also disappeared. The bartender may have given him a passing thought or so in the ensuing weeks, but certainly wasted no time in sympathizing with a man who was robbed and then whipped in a fair fight. The following pay day he had cause to remember. The man was back, and this time he had a friend with him. The second stranger didn't drink much, he sat most of the time and watched the door. He had a pronounced cauliflower ear, his nose was flat as a fritter, and his knuckles were gnarled and broken. He had "pug" written all over him, and although fifty pounds lighter than his embittered companion, he still outweighed John by 30 pounds. To top it all, he appeared wise in the craft and wiles of the ring, and a novice could guess that bar-room brawls were definitely his dish.

As the bartender watched the two men, something clicked in his mind and he thought he saw a picture. Very quietly he took off his apron, turned to his helper and said, "I'll be back purty quick. You hold 'er down 'til I git back." He slipped out the door and began a round of all of the saloons asking the same question, "Seen Jack Sornberger in town?"

In the eighth bar he found a lead, and five minutes later he located John and ten of his crew in a saloon. He drew

73

the boy aside and in a few sentences told him what sort of a pot was stewing, and John's eyes lit up with glee.

"Pug, huh?" he asked.

"Yep," said the bartender, "and plenty tough!"

"Get the floor cleared" said John, "so I'll have plenty room to move around. Get the tables out of the way and the chairs up against the wall, and in ten minutes I'll come in."

The bartender returned in haste to set the stage, and ten minutes later nine men walked in, all of them carrying axe handles and peavies. Without a word they surrounded the jack whom John had licked a month before, and at once their champion stepped through the door. He came up to the bar, took off his coat, faced the pug and said, "All right, here I am. Let's see what you have besides a busted beak and a twisted ear!"

The surprised gladiator came off the chair like a jack-in-the-box. He was confused by the suddenness of the challenge. He had expected to have to spend minutes picking a fight. But he recognized an invitation, and hurled himself at the lesser man. He brought up a haymaker that would have felled an ox. The only trouble was that John was not where the punch landed. He had spun on his toes and the mighty wallop whistled through thin air. Before the man could recover, John hit him three times, and that fellow knew he had been hit each time! It taught him caution. He tucked his chin down into his shoulder and carefully began to feel John out with a straight left. A dozen light blows he landed before he was sure he had the range. Then he uncorked the finishing punch, and the fight ended.

But not as the professional had planned. Once again John was inches away when the fatal blow arrived where he had been but was now no more! The force of the swing threw the battler off balance and left him wide open. John stepped in with a graceful twist and hit the pug with every ounce of muscle and bone in his rangy frame. The pug went down like a dead tree in a wind, and never moved when they picked him up and carried him out. There was a stillness in the saloon that could be felt when John walked up to the big lumberjack and said, "Friend of yours?"

"Nope" said the fellow, "just a hired hand!"

"Looks like you're going to have to find you a new employee," John suggested.

The other man looked him in the eye a long minute and answered, "I don't reckon so, friend. I guess I lost all interest in getting that job done. She looks like too big a contract for one man to handle, and I don't like a big crew!"

John grinned and replied, "I believe you used the word 'friend.' In this neck of the woods friends buy each other a drink. Have one with me?"

The big man laughed, put his arm around John and said, "I guess I'd better, come to think of it. I believe I paid for several last time we was together."

A wave of laughter, whoops, yells and genial blasphemy swept over the saloon and the usual orgy began, to end only when the crew was busted, sick and stupid from excess, sadly wending its way back to the camp again.

Three days later, as John was busy in the kitchen, the door opened and the defeated prize-fighter came in. John casually picked up a cleaver and watched him approach. When he got close the visitor said, "Put it down, pal, you don't need it. Not with me or any other *one* man I ever saw in action. Where did you learn to fight?" John said, "I never learned. I just picked it up here and there mostly by practice."

The fighter nodded and said, "Any chance to get a job in this camp?"

Suspiciously John inquired, "Just why do you want to work here?"

The boxer said, "I'd sort of like to help you practice. Maybe I could help you pick up one or two little things you ain't seen yet."

So John gained a gifted tutor in an old art, and in three months added a real knowledge of ring craft to his native ability and strength. Once again the woods began to echo with the name of a great fighter, and the rival camps sent their best men to find out if he was as good as rumor reported. They came down from Great Rainy, Bigfork, from Michigan and from Wisconsin, and John met and vanquished them all. He was the idol of an area of a quarter of a million square miles, where manhood was measured chiefly in terms of fighting ability. None of this was very pleasing to the elder Sornberger, who felt that his family name was being degraded, and his protests and denunciations became increasingly frequent and more bitter. So, to save himself further family difficulty, John decided to take an alias and began to call himself "Jack McWilliams," under which name he fought his professional battles.

The fame of this new "Bull of the Woods" reached the Twin Cities in a brief time, and two noted fight promoters decided to capitalize on John. The men were partners: one ran a boxing academy and was called "Professor" Lewis, the other was the notorious Tom Beaver. They had to decide whether they would throw John to the lions and make a quick clean-up, or nurse him along for a larger number of fights and reap a greater profit in the long run. There were thousands of jacks who would bet their shirts on their champion, and the promoters felt sure they could get a top notch boxer who could lick the lad from the woods. Their profit, of course, would come primariy from the money they could post on the betting books.

They gave considerable thought to the matter, and after watching John in two fights, they decided he had all the requirements of a ring champion, *if* he was able to stand up under a beating and not lose his nerve. His one fault was that he won all his fights so fast the other fellow got little chance to hurt him! So the question uppermost in their minds was, "Can he *take* it?" To settle this matter they took a typically direct approach. One of the odd characters who hung around their establishment was a tough brawler, who went by the euphonious name of "Cannibal Jones" because of his deplorable habit of biting his opponents in a rough house. Many a fighting shanty man went about with a mangled ear as a souvenir of an affair with Cannibal Jones. In a clinch he endeavored earnestly to chew off any appendage he could clamp his teeth on.

So the genial promoters hired Jones for a modest fee and took him up to Grand Rapids to help them in a bit of laboratory research. He was given his instructions, the trap was set, and they waited for the victim to walk into it. They had picked the ideal time! Payday! And they had chosen the proper place—John's favorite saloon. When the boy entered with his cronies the promoters pointed him out to Jones and said, "Go ahead!"

John was standing at the bar when Jones pushed in next to him and said, "You're Jack McWilliams, ain't you?" Shrewdly his victim sized him up, and didn't like what he saw. The warrior was scarred and battered and mean looking, and John smelled a mouse that was half as big as a barn. He didn't like any part of what he saw, and didn't intend to be caught in close quarters. So he backed away until he was in the clear. The crowd recognized a familiar pattern and got out of the way in a hurry, giving John all the space he needed for fast foot work. The woods were full of out-laws and desperate men who preferred a gun or a knife to fists, and who used brass knuckles when a club was not available, and a wise battler with a reputation to maintain could not afford to take chances. So John kept his mouth shut until he was set where he could operate to best advantage, and then replied, "Yes, I'm Jack

McWilliams. Who are you?" "I'm the feller" the bully retorted, "who's looking for Jack McWilliams."

With no further warning he swung at John, who shifted and ducked. The blow missed him, and left the challenger wide open. John brought up a swift and powerful uppercut which connected with the chin of Jones, who promptly measured his length on the floor. He lay there quietly for a moment, getting his head clear, while John crouched over him, all set to sock him again as he was getting up. But Jones fooled him. Instead of getting to his feet he rolled over and sunk his teeth in John's left leg just above the ankle. John gave a howl of rage and pain, and kicked with all of his strength at Jones' face. He connected with a spattering sound which brought a yell from the crowd and forced Jones to roll over, but not before he had literally bitten a piece out of his enemy's leg. As he rolled he was in position to set his teeth in John's right leg, and immediately got the other foot in his face. So they danced and rolled over the floor, Cannibal Jones doing his best to chew the flesh off the dancing boxer, and John trying mightily to kick the face off the man on the floor. The feet won, and Jones was booted into insensibility, but not before the floor was slick with blood. John wore the scars of that hideous conflict to his grave—Jones never fought again.

While the swampers were carrying Jones out to deposit him in the gutter, John turned to his cronies and said, "Come on boys, let's have another drink!" They cheered him and rushed to the bar where "Professor" Lewis slid in next to John.

"Jack," he said, "you're bleeding like a stuck pig. Better see the saw-bones and get those legs bandaged."

"Later, maybe," said John. "Right now I got some heavy drinking to do."

"Now!" said the Professor, "and you are through with heavy drinking for a long time."

John pulled back with his fists cocked and asked, "Who are you to be giving me orders?"

Lewis answered very quietly, "I'm the man you're working for now, and you will follow my orders. They are for your own good."

This took John off his feet, and he said, "So I'm working for you, am I? What for?"

The professor said, "For hundreds of dollars where you are getting dimes now—*thousands* of dollars if you are smart and do just as I tell you."

The smell of big money intrigued John, and he quieted down and said, "Tell me some more about this." Lewis said, "I'll give you the whole story as soon as we get those legs tied up. You are too valuable a man to take a chance on blood-poisoning from dirty teeth. Let's go see the Doc."

John suffered himself to be led out, and began a new chapter of his life. For eight years he was to be cock of the walk, champion in two divisions of the ring, the idol of the sporting fraternity, the winner of 127 ring battles in a day when they *fought* and did not box. Years during which he rolled in easy money. He could not know this at the moment, but he was in very truth Adventure's Darling and Fortune's Protegé. He had his feet planted on the threshold of fame, and the coffers of the future were opening to pour a golden stream into his purse—which would as promptly pour the treasure out again! Barely 18 years of age, he "had the world by the tail, with a down-hill pull."

So he put himself under the tutelage and control of Lewis and Beaver, who later reaped a fortune in payment for their foresight and shrewdness. They afterwards told John that they had paid Cannibal Jones ten dollars to start that fight and try him out for courage and stamina, and John laughed with glee as he offered to refund the money on the grounds that it was a lucky break for him. And at

the time it seemed as though it really was—quite the finest
thing a young fighter could desire.

# The Prodigal's Progress

# CHAPTER II

# The Prodigal's Progress

Now began a life of hard work and rigid discipline for John. His mentors and new owners were determined to capitalize on their find to the utmost. They put their protegé through a series of Turkish baths day after day, sweating the alcohol out of his system as they waited for his legs to heal. Their new fighter was rangy and weighed only 122 pounds, so they tried to put more weight on him. John revelled in an avalanche of thick, juicy steaks, he had milk and butter and eggs until he said, "They come out my ears," but he still retained his slenderness. Lewis decided it was due to his youth, and so they planned to start John in the lightweight class, where his height and reach would give him tremendous advantage. Lewis took personal charge of his boxing technique, and John was a very apt pupil. He already had a punch that would fell an ox, and hours of slugging a sand bag made it even more lethal. When he had been training two months, his sponsors could not find a man his weight who would box with him, so he had to train against middleweights and welters.

Road work built up his wind and developed his legs until he was in the pink of condition and restless for a fight. But his managers said, "No" and put him back on the treadmill. He realized that they knew what they were doing, and he cooperated, working like a galley-slave. Out on the road before dawn jogging and running five to seven miles every morning. Then a shower, a rub down, and a breakfast fit for two men. Next came a session with the Professor, who patiently and skilfully corrected every fault of balance, foot work, and defense.

Then the showers again, a rub down, and lunch. An hour on the cot while his meal digested, then his sparring and wrestling partners earned their daily pay—and *how* they earned it! John never learned to pull a punch. When he hit it was for keeps, and his hired help came and went in a constant two-way stream. The gleam of satisfaction brightened in the promoters' eyes as the weeks fled by, and avarice intensified the shine. Finally the Professor decided it was time to launch "Jack McWilliams" on the sporting seas, and a bout was arranged.

His first opponent was a promising lad of twenty years, who had six wins to his credit and seemed on the way up. The bout was well advertised, the house was a sell out, and the odds were three to one against John. This disturbed him so little he borrowed a hundred dollars from Beaver and bet it on himself to win!

The elder Sornberger was working near Grand Rapids at the time, acting as foreman in the camp where John had worked. Three days before the fight Mr. Buckman was in camp, and he said to his foreman, "I see your son is fighting in St. Paul this week. Are you going down to watch him?"

The stern old gentleman said, "You are mistaken, sir, I have no son in the prize ring."

Mr. Buckman was puzzled and said, "Why, sure you have. I mean John. He's fighting Friday night."

"No," said Mr. Sornberger, "that's Jack McWilliams. As far as I know or care John Sornberger is dead!"

So in literal truth John had left his father's home. This meant very little to him at the time. For the first time in his life he had more than one suit of clothes, his pockets were plentifully supplied with money, painted women were flattered to be seen with him, and like every other prodigal in past history he never even dreamed of a future swine pen where a ragged man fought for husks.

An hour before the fight, the Professor came to John's room to escort him to the arena, where he was to act as second to his boy and advise him through the ordeal. When he entered the room, John was ready; hat and overcoat on, boxing trunks and shoes in a small bag. Lewis gestured to a chair and said, "Sit down while I tell you something." When John was sprawled in the chair the Professor said in a quiet voice, "I just threw away five thousand dollars!" He paused to let that sink in, then continued quietly, "A gambler offered to bet me even money you would be knocked out in the first round. I asked him what odds he would give if I'd bet a thousand dollars you would knock out *his* boy in the first round, and he offered five to one. I didn't take the bet."

John sat up in alert interest, and said, "Why? Didn't you think I could do it?"

"Yes," said Lewis, "I am reasonably sure you can. That's why I said I threw away five thousand."

John was thoroughly puzzled and said, "I don't get it. Why didn't you take the bet?"

Lewis said, "How did you learn to read and write?"

It took John a moment to get his mind off the subject, and then he said, "Why, teachers showed me how, I guess."

Lewis shook his head in a decided negative and tried again, "Let's put it this way. You are a good shot, aren't you?"

John nodded.

"How did you learn to shoot?"

"Practice!"

Lewis said no more for a minute, then John began to grin. The Professor watched his smile, leaned over and put his hand on John's knee and said, "That's the only way *anybody* ever learns *anything*. When the teacher showed you how to read you had to do it so you could learn to do it. When you got a gun in your hand you had to shoot it so you could learn to shoot it. It's the same with boxing, or fighting. You are a good boy, I've given you lessons, but you will never know whether you learned them or not 'til you try them out. This is no sparring partner you face tonight. This is a tough kid who wants to tear your block off in one round. Don't let him do it! This fight is advertised for ten rounds. I want you to *practice* for the first six of them. See if you remember what we've tried to show you. Here's a chance to practice, and get paid for it. Start *fighting* in the seventh round—finish him in the eighth. The customers have paid thousands of dollars to get in tonight. Let's be smart and give them a good show so they will come back the next time and pay us more money!"

John turned this over in his mind for a full five minutes, and the Professor waited patiently for his decision. Then John nodded, reached out to shake the Professor's hand and said, "Mr. Lewis, you are a very smart man! And I am a lucky pup to have you for a friend and teacher. You are the boss from now on. You tell me what to do, and I'll bust a gut trying!"

Lewis smiled with real pleasure and said, "All right, son, let's go," and they stepped out for the arena.

The fight was a sell out. Hundreds of admirers had come down from the Itasca woods to see John in his ring *debut*, and their flood of money had changed the odds until even money was going begging. The boy was perfectly cool. He was just doing what he loved to do, and getting paid for it beside! He went to his drafty dressing room, stripped, got into his ring togs and a bathrobe, and lay on a table completely relaxed while a trainer kneaded his muscles and his seconds bandaged his hands. When the call came he got up and started confidently for the ring. It was just a fight to him, and the only difference was in the setting. A ring instead of a bar room, and a referee to keep more than one man from jumping him at a time.

When he came down the aisle the jacks went wild. They were far outnumbered by the local boy's following, but they had better lungs and bigger voices. The din was so great no single sound could be discerned as an intelligible sentence, and John just grinned and nodded as his handlers shepherded him to the center of the arena. He climbed through the ropes, submitted to the scrutiny of his bandages by his opponent's seconds, who were looking for thin sheets of lead wound in them, or plaster of Paris to reinforce the cloth covering his knuckles. In those days anything went you could get away with, even a horse shoe in the gloves—for luck. Then they tied a hard pair of five-ounce gloves on his hands, and John was ready for the fray.

He leaned back in his corner and studied his adversary. He saw a man three inches shorter than he, but five pounds heavier; his face was brutally marked with the scars of previous fights. He had short arms but powerful shoulders, and John unconsciously decided he'd never clinch with that fellow. The referee called them to the center, gave them the usual instructions, and said, "Shake hands, and when the bell rings come out fighting." John put out his glove to shake hands, and the local boy spit on it and turned away. John grinned. This was more like it! He had been afraid the bout would turn out to be a cross between a boxing match and a dancing exhibition, but this lad wanted a *fight*. That was more in line with John's desires, so he decided to accommodate the chap.

When the bell sounded John went across the ring like an arrow from a bow, and caught his opponent flat-footed. He hit him three times before the local lad got set, and the fight almost ended right there. The favorite folded to his knees and rolled over sideways, and the referee began to

87

count over the prostrate form. At that time there was none of this silly custom of going to a neutral corner when a man was down. John stood over him, ready to slug as soon as the fighter got to his knees. But the lad had been there before. At the count of "seven" he reached out a hooking arm which swept John's feet out from under him and brought him to his knees facing his rising enemy. The crowd howled with glee as the two lads knelt and exchanged a dozen blows, before they rolled apart and came to their feet.

John waded in eagerly and swapped wallop for wallop until the bell sounded. He had been floored three times, his opponent had been down five times, and the first round was definitely his. The spectators were delirious with joy as the seconds hustled the principals to their corners for the minute rest, and began to work on them. Lewis swabbed John's bleeding nose, wiped the sweat from his brow and said, "Nice work, son, you are a credit to my teaching. You certainly showed that boy how you can stay away and box, just like I told you to do in the room."

John was stricken. All the elation and wild excitement fled, leaving him cold and chagrined. He said in real contrition, "Mr. Lewis, I forgot! Honest, I did, but I'll remember now. I'll practice, like you told me to."

The Professor smiled, patted John on the shoulder and said, "Sure, I know. A fellow sometimes goes off at half cock. Now go in there and stick your left in his mug and don't take it out for a whole round."

John did exactly that. The other man rushed to the center and John dodged and let him pass. He rushed back again and once more John was three feet away. Exasperated, he dropped his hands and said, "Come on and fight!" and John hit him three times before he could get his hands up. For most of the round John held him off, cutting him up with a stabbing left. Then, in apparent disgust, the cagey fighter dropped his arms, started to turn away, and turned right back with his right arm coming over in a sizzling cross. John walked right into it. He had plunged in to hit his man as he turned away, and got walloped as the lad turned back! He saw fireworks, and heard the referee saying "three" when the bell rang. His seconds dragged him to the corner, and for the first time in his life John found out what smelling salts smell like! A cold towel on the back of his neck, pungent liniment on his belly muscles, and when the gong rang his head was clear and he was fighting mad.

When he started that third round he went out to fight. He met his opponent in the center of the ring, and anchored himself right there. He blocked and rolled every punch and used his long arms to whittle the heavier man down to where he had about enough. Every time his adversary tried to clinch, John straightened him with an uppercut, and when the round ended that fight was in the bag.

As Lewis worked on him during the short rest, he said, "All right, son, I don't guess you'll ever be a boxer. No use painting a lily. You were born a fighter and you'd better just fight. I found out what I want to know. From now on the fight is your own. Finish him up any *time* you can, any *way* you can."

With glee John heard those words, and when the bell rand for round four he leaped to the fray. The more experienced man knew he had been boxed off his feet that third round, and was expecting the same tactics. He had planned to rush John as soon as the bell rang. John had the same idea. They met in the middle of the square circle, and John uncorked. Words could not describe the pandemonium that reigned in the arena! Sheer frenzy gripped the fight-mad mob until their screams were incoherent. They were certainly getting their money's worth! In the middle of the fourth round John got his chance, and landed a perfect punch right on the button.

His opponent went down glassy-eyed and dead to the world. It was ten minutes before they brought him around.

The next day the Twin Cities were ringing with cheers for Jack McWilliams, the new star in the firmament of sport. It also dripped with Squirrel Whiskey, Panther Sweat, Nigger Head Gin and plain alcohol as the elated jacks blew their winnings across the bars: none of them stopping for rest until their last dollar was gone. Then each drunken wretch would fall on the floor or in an alley to sleep it off—later to rouse himself and wander back to his job in the woods.

Mr. Buckman had seen the fight, and came to the hotel next morning to have breakfast with John, who was higher than a kite riding the winds of elation. He had collected three hundred dollars as his share of the purse, won another three hundred on a bet, and had money pressed on him by exuberant winners who jammed currency in his pockets as they roared from saloon to saloon. He had never had a hundred dollars at one time in his life before, and now he counted his assets on the breakfast table, and had a full thousand dollars. The older man watched him and asked, "John, is this another case of 'easy come, easy go?' What are you going to do with that stake?" John made two even piles of the money, slid five hundred dollars across the table and said, "Will you please take that to my father, and tell him I want him to buy something for himself or the farm?"

Mr. Buckman hesitated, knowing the stern code and rigid standards of the old man, whose rectitude and Christian character were a tradition in the woods. He didn't want to hurt the boy's feelings, so he said, "I'm not sure he would take it, John, knowing how you got it. Maybe you had better wait and give it to him when you see him."

But John insisted, and the lumber king put the money in his pocket. Four weeks later, when he came to

Minneapolis to see John in his third fight, he drew him aside and returned the money. John asked, "What did he say?"

Buckman replied, "Your father said, 'I have no son. And if I did have, I'd take no part of the wages of sin and violence. Let Jack McWilliams' dirty money perish with him. I'll have no part nor lot in either.' I'm sorry, son, but I thought I'd best tell you the truth and save you future grief."

John's mouth twisted into a bitter curse, he turned on his heel and went away. The first saloon he came to he burst in through the door and hollered, "Up to the bar, boys, the drinks are on me." He slapped the five hundred dollars on the bar, snarled, "Drink it up, you hogs!" and stalked out.

That was the last overture the prodigal ever made to his father. He felt that the door of his house had been slammed in his face, and that ended his filial duty. When next he came to his father he came as a suppliant and a fugitive from justice, but that was many years later.

In the meantime he rode high, wide, and handsome. He wore the sportiest clothes money could buy, he lived in the finest hotels of the region, he travelled over a half dozen states, and fought all comers. In a year he had won the lightweight championship and held it for another twelve months. Then he was too heavy for that division, so he went up into the middleweight class. He again won the championship and held it for six years. In that time he fought 127 ring battles and was an easy victor in every contest. The saga of Jack McWilliams can still be read in the sports columns of old newspapers of that day. The press idolized him, as he was always "good copy" and generous with passes, free drinks, meals for the boys, and cash loans when they were busted.

Then he came to the end of the primrose path, and met the two adversaries who defeated him: John Barleycorn and the champion of Australia, who invaded the Northwest because he had licked everyone else who would fight him. The bout was a natural; two undefeated men, tough, rough, and ruthless were to battle to a knock out. The fight-loving loggers would have walked a thousand miles to see such a bout.

John had been slipping, because of pride and self-esteem. He refused to train, stating complacently that he could lick any man alive, and didn't need any more practice. For six months past he had been dallying with bad liquor and worse women, and was woefully out of condition. Lewis did everything he could to shake him out of his vanity, but failed utterly. In disgust the Professor went out and quietly bet every dollar he had on the Australian to win.

When John entered the ring for what was destined to be his last fight, he had already defeated himself. He was burned out with liquor and lust, and his stamina was gone. From the first minute it was apparent that he had met his master. To eliminate the gory details, it is sufficient to recall that his opponent broke John's nose in the first round, and his left arm in the second one. True to his fighting nature, John never told his seconds his arm was broken, and he fought doggedly through the third and fourth rounds with that broken bone nauseating him every time he moved his left. In the fifth round the Australian Flash broke John's jaw with a mighty wallop, and he was out for a quarter of an hour. So sturdy was his fighting heart, when he came to fifteen minutes later in the dressing room, he struggled off the table and began swinging at the doctor who was binding up his wounds! He thought he was still in the ring.

Three months of recuperation used up his share of that last purse, and he came out of the hospital flat broke. He was too proud to go back to fighting preliminaries when he had reigned as champion for so long, and he drifted back into the woods. Once again a Buckman camp put him on the payroll as a Bull Cook, and Jack McWilliams came to the sordid end of his transient day of glory. His glad raiment was gone, his popularity had waned, and he had to sweat for his daily bread—*and* his nightly liquor. Now he drank whenever he had the price. Being used to easy money he was not content with the small wage of toil, and took the next step down.

That fall he went to North Dakota as cook with a thrashing team, which was working in the vast grain fields of that state. It was wild and rugged, but dry under local option in the vicinity where John's crew worked. When the crew was paid, they headed for one of the many blind pigs at the town of Fingle, North Dakota. The place was roaring with drunken harvest hands, the mayor and the sheriff were playing poker with some other prominent citizens in the back room, and the dive keeper was taking in money with both hands. It was a nice set-up for a footpad, and John saw a chance for easy pickings.

He was armed, as usual, with a Colt .45, and he went outside in the dark, took off his neck bandanna, and cut two slits in it for eyes. He tucked that part of the handkerchief down under his shirt collar, re-entered the saloon, and waited until the men started drifting out. Soon John's crew was the only group left, and he suggested that they go, also. Laughing and whooping in drunken glee they roared on toward camp together. John, who had stayed sober, darted back without being missed. He peered in through the door, and saw the proprietor stuffing cash in his wallet, which he put in his hip pocket. John pulled his bandanna up under his hat to hide his face, peering out through the slits he had cut in the cloth. His own mother could not have recognized him.

With gun in hand he slipped up behind the bootlegger, and when the man turned he was looking right down the bore of a Colt .45, which must have appeared to him to be about the diameter of a washtub! John had one finger on his lips as a warning, and the blind pigger was too smart to cry out in the face of that pistol. John went to the cash register and made the man turn his back while he cleaned out the till. The victim was glad he had put most of the big money in his wallet, but his happiness was of short duration. John put the gun in his back, lifted his coat tail, and took the wallet. He motioned the helpless publican into a store room, locked the door and sprinted. As he passed the railway station, he wrapped the gun and the loot in the bandanna, tossed the package under the platform, and ran after the crew. So fast had he worked, he caught up with them before they reached camp.

The sheriff was boiling along in their wake, and I mean boiling! He was so wrathful over the insult of having the groggery held up while he was in it, he could hardly think. He lined the men up and searched them all. There weren't two dollars left in the crowd, and no one had a gun. John smelled as bad as the rest of the crew, and when the sheriff searched him he lurched and swayed, and hiccoughed in his face. The disgusted officer went on, searching all the other crews and camps for days before he gave up. He finally decided that the job had been done by a transient who had gotten well away, so he went back to playing poker.

John stayed on the job until the hue and cry died out, then he developed a strange malady. The doctor couldn't diagnose it, he put it down to "bad liquor and general cussedness" and went back to town. Two days later John said he was really too sick to work and asked for his time.

Paid off, he went back to Fingle to catch a night train back to Minnesota. Before the train came, he crawled under the depot platform, recovered the swag and his gun, and went home a thousand dollars richer. Also another step down in his prodigal's progress! Now he was a thief, wanted by the law! This was a real moral toboggan slide he was on, and the day was not far distant when children would flee in terror when the dreaded Jack McWilliams came down the street, twisting his heart with pain at the idea that boys and girls, whom he loved, feared him because of his wild ways and black reputation.

Like all prodigals, he started out by justifying himself. He had a small gang of elect ruffians with whom he worked, and they specialized in robbing blind pigs and high-jacking saloons. He had a glib explanation for his conduct, which I can give you best in his own words—"A blind pigger is a robber to begin with. He sells poison liquor to a man and gets him blind and stupid drunk, and steals the rest of the poor devil's money outright. Now, a thief has no right to money he stole, so if a second fellow steals it from the thief, he ain't really doing any wrong. The wrong was done in stealing from the first man, who was the rightful owner, and I wouldn't do that. I only took it from the thief who stole it, and I used a gun and not a bottle of poisoned booze—so there is really nothing immoral in what I did, the way I did it!" And he not only believed that queer philosophy himself, but he actually persuaded his gang to believe it, and they looked upon themselves as Robin Hoods, more than as highwaymen.

One night in Bemidji, about six months after John took to the Hoot Owl Trail, he held up a bootlegger who was armed and elected to shoot it out. John could easily have killed him as he drew, but instead he shot him through the shoulder. The man dropped his pistol and surrendered his cash, but an officer of the law had heard the shot and came running. He opened fire on John, who promptly took to his heels down a dark alley. Every time the deputy got too close, the fleeing man fired a shot past his ear and slowed him down, and got away safely. But he had been recognized, and the next day there was a warrant out for the arrest of "Jack McWilliams." John fled to the one sure refuge of the hunted man: he took a job as cook deep in the woods and dropped out of sight for weeks.

But he was active in his spare time during this enforced stretch of labor: he robbed every blind pig and bootlegger in a radius of a hundred miles. Forced to flee from a posse which was after him, he slipped down the Mississippi to the Twin Cities, leaving a half dozen warrants behind him, and the echoes of many gun fights. The dives of the Twin Cities gave him rich harvests until the law drove him out, and he went back to North Dakota again. He broke his journey at Bemidji, where he robbed a saloon and left a furious sheriff swearing out *new* warrants. A few months later he fled back into Northern Minnesota, two jumps ahead of North Dakota peace officers. Again he passed through Bemidji on the way to Wisconsin, and once more he left his imprint in passing. By the end of that year he was wanted in four states, and every county in Northern Minnesota was looking for him.

John had a contempt for the sheriff of Bemidji, whom he said was "yellow." Several times the two men had met face to face when the officer was alone, and he carefully failed to recognize John. One such occasion occurred when John was unarmed, and half drunk, spoiling for a fight. The outlaw walked up to him and said, "When a peace officer, wearing a big star and a gun, meets a wanted man who ain't even armed, it's the officer's duty to march that man off to jail! I ain't got a gun. Why don't you take *me*?" The sheriff was a very lonely man at that moment. Either he didn't believe John when he said he had no gun, or the terrible reputation of the desperate outlaw overawed him, because he just turned on his heel and walked away!

But the experience must have rankled, because he began a quiet investigation to see why John kept returning to Bemidji. Nobody knew what the sheriff was up to as he asked apparently unrelated questions, but after a few days of diligent digging he turned up with the astonishing fact that John had a "common law" wife in the town, and spent days and nights with her. So the wily officer laid a trap, and the next time John came to the house the sheriff was waiting hidden in the bushes. He had taken off his boots and stood in his socks, so when John appeared the peace officer sneaked up behind him and stuck a gun in his back. I heard John tell his experience many times, and he said the officer was so scared he was shaking like a leaf. This frightened John, who was afraid the gun would go off in the excitement, so he surrendered and suffered himself to be disarmed. The sheriff was so excited he forgot his boots, and marched John off to jail, the law still being in his socks!

The sheriff's brother was the city marshal, and as such was in charge of the jail. They locked John up in a cell, and took several drinks to celebrate the event. In an hour it was all over Bemidji that the notorious outlaw was safe behind the bars. There was considerable betting, as to his probable fate, life imprisonment and hanging being the most popular ideas. John lay in his cell and rested, with the marshal coming every half hour to be sure his famous captive was still in safe keeping.

When midnight came, John called the marshal and said, "Do me a favor, will you?"

The marshal cursed him and said, "NO!" Then curiosity got the upper hand, and he asked, "What sort of favor?"

The prisoner grinned and answered, "I want you to go to the nearest saloon and tell the boys Jack McWilliams wants a dozen of them to come stand under his cell window. I want to tell the whole town how your yellow rat of a brother hid behind a woman's skirts with his shoes off, to stick a gun in a man's back, because he was afraid to face an unarmed man. Then I want to tell them how his dirty rat of a brother *hid* in the jail until I was locked up, so he wouldn't be in any danger in case I made a break. I want to tell them that your whole family is a miserable collection of inbred degenerates, and that half of the crime in this town is committed by the Law itself. Why, I know for a fact that you have burglarized half of the stores in this town when you were supposed to be walking a beat, you dirty — — — — !"

While John was still cursing him with every vile name he knew, the marshal, frantic with rage, was struggling to get the cell open, shouting, "I'll jam your dirty lies down your — — — — throat!"

His key finally worked, and the angry man hurled himself at John, who was set for just such a chance. He could still slug, and one swift uppercut with his right took the foolish, half drunken officer on the chin, and he went out like a light. As he hit the floor, the outlaw kicked him behind the ear to be sure he would stay out, calmly picked up the keys, walked out, and locked the marshal in the cell.

He went to the front office and searched a desk until he found his gun, some money, and an extra box of cartridges. Then he coolly went out and locked the front door behind him, and headed for the woods where he was safe from pursuit. He was ten miles away when he gave the keys a mighty fling into the brush, and it was late the next morning before the marshal's plight was discovered. The whole town howled with laughter while two blacksmiths used up their whole stock of files getting the jail keeper out of his own cell. There were no spare keys.

By back trails John worked his way over to the Mississippi, where he had a hideout he had often used before. This was the cabin of an old negro, whom John had often befriended. The old man would have sold his soul to repay the outlaw, for one of the strangest things about this wild marauder was his love for the downtrodden and the poor. He would fight for the underdog as a matter of principle, and steal from those who had to give to those who were in need. Many a barrel of flour and side of salt port had found its way to that small cabin on the bank of the upper Mississippi, and it had in turn been a place of refuge for a fleeing man. So John knew he would be safely hidden until the hue and cry blew over.

But luck was against him, and as he slipped through Grand Rapids, some one spotted him in the light from a window and recognized him. There was a substantial reward on his head, so the informer ran to the sheriff with the news. This man was of a different kidney from the Bemidji officer, and he set out immediately on John's trail.

The cabin was a few hundred yards from the mill, and across the river. The stream had been dammed up to make a shallow millpond which was then full of logs and John got across in the night by leaping from log to log, an easy trick for any jack. He slipped quietly into the cabin, curled up on the floor, and went to sleep. When the owner awoke next morning he was surprised to see that he had company. But his pleasure was greater than his astonishment, and soon he had the coffee pot boiling, bacon frying, and flapjacks ready for the pan. John had been forty-eight hours without food, and he did justice to the meal. Then he leaned against the wall and told his dusky friend how he broke jail. The old man laughed until the tears ran, and assured John he was safe and bade him just keep out of sight.

In the meantime the sheriff had been narrowing his search to a small area, and while talking to a hand at the mill, which was shut down for repairs, he learned for the first time that John and the old darky were pals. He smelled a mouse, and asked for two men to help him. A couple volunteered, put pistols in their pockets, were sworn in as deputies, and went to aid the sheriff in the arrest.

As they crossed the river the negro spotted them, and John was warned. The two went into the cabin and closed the door. John tried to induce his host to go out and leave him alone so as to avoid trouble with the law, but the old man was stubborn, and said, "No, Mister Jack, you is my friend. You come to my house for refuge, and I aims to provide it."

"All right," John said, "if that's the way you want it. Now, I'll tell you what you do. They can't come in your house without a warrant, so you refuse to open the door unless they have one. It might not help, but at least it will gain us time to plan, if we can think of any way out."

The cabin had only the one front door, and one rear window which faced the river and the millpond.

When the sheriff arrived in the clearing, he posted his two men where they could watch the window, drew his gun, and pounded on the closed door.

Following instructions to the letter, Tom asked in a quavering voice, "Who's there, and whadda you want?"

"This is the law," thundered the sheriff, "and we know who you have in there. Open up or I'll break down the door."

"Ain't no call to do that," the cabin owner said in a placating tone of voice. "I'm alone in here, and I ain't going to open the door."

"I'll give you just thirty seconds," the sheriff said grimly. "*And then I'm coming in, shooting*!"

"You got a search warrant?" Tom inquired.

There was a long silence, then the sheriff tried to put over a bluff. "I don't need a search warrant to arrest an outlaw, and I've got *several* warrants for him. You open up or I'll put *you* in jail for harboring a fugitive from justice."

"Ain't no outlaws in here," the darky insisted. "This is my house, and you can't come in without a search warrant. I don't know much, but I know *that* much. You git you a warrant and I'll open up."

The sheriff began to curse with exasperation, but Tom didn't waver. Finally the officer said, "All right, I'll *get* a

100

search warrant, and another one for you. I'll put you in jail so deep and for so long you'll never get out!"

He turned away from the door and posted his two deputies so they covered the two exits. One man was squarely in front of the door, and the other crouched under the rear window where he was safe from a pistol shot through the glass. "You two men hold your pistols in your hands," said the sheriff, "and if he shows himself let him have it. He's wanted dead or alive, and I'd sooner see him dead than alive. I'll be back with warrants in forty minutes, and if he gets away I'll skin the two of you."

He rushed off to cross the river and hasten back to town, while John rubbed his hands with satisfaction. He called Tom over to where he was in the corner, and said, "Now listen carefully and do just what I tell you." They put their heads together and John talked for five minutes in the darky's ear. Old Tom shook with silent laughter, nodded his grey head, and said, "Mr. Jack, you is a *smart man*. But how *you* gonna git outa here?"

John said, "You unlock the door quietly, so the deputy won't hear you, and keep your hand on the knob. When I holler 'now' you fling it wide open and get out of the way."

Tom signified his accord, and John went to the rear of the small cabin and braced his back and his hands against the wall. He shouted, "Now!" and Tom flung the door wide upon its hinges. John was in motion like a fullback carrying the ball, and he shot out of that door like a stone from a catapult. The deputy turned as the door opened, and John hit him full in the chest with his shoulder. The man went one way and his gun the other, and John cut around the cabin on one wheel, wide open, leaving the guardian of the front door flat on his back wondering what had hit him.

The second man had heard the commotion, of course, and came dashing around the corner to investigate. He was expected. John met him with a stiff arm that turned him end for end and didn't even slow the fleeing man in his course. In a dozen jumps, hitting on all six, John reached the river and went in head first. Before the dazed guards had regained their weapons their prey was wading across the river under the screen of logs. Half way over he came to a point just chin deep, the surface completely covered with logs. He stuck his face up to the air between two logs, and just stood there completely concealed. The deputies emptied their pistols at the ripples covering the spot where John had hit the water, never realizing that he was fifty yards away.

This was the stalemate the sheriff faced when he returned with his nice, legal warrants, and a madder peace officer never wore a badge. He gathered the few men at the mill, armed them with pikes, and started pushing logs from both sides. They never came within sight of the prey. John slowly and quietly shifted his position when he needed to, his sharp eyes keeping watch between the logs. The sheriff was obstinate and refused to quit until darkness made further search useless. Then he called off his men and withdrew.

John, fearing a trap, stayed where he was until he judged it was close to midnight. Then he worked his way down the pond to a bank and crawled out. There was an old, disused tote road which he remembered, and he crawled out and started walking up that road. But the sheriff was foxy, also, and he too knew of that road. Putting himself in the outlaw's place, he reasoned what he would do, and stationed himself up that road. Alert, but not expecting a trap, John walked along at a good pace, not realizing that his shoes, full of water, were going "squish, squash" at every step.

The keen ears of the peace officer heard the sound, which was just what he was waiting for. When he judged by the noise that John was close, he drew his gun, stepped out in the path, and cried, "Put up your hands and stand still. I've got you covered."

John whirled like a flash and took off like a jack rabbit with a wolf at its tail. He flung himself to the left as he ran, the sheriff opening fire. The outlaw jumped to the right, and the sheriff fired again. John, realizing that his noisy shoes were betraying him, slid into a clump of brush, took out his pocket knife and cut the strings with two quick strokes. He slipped them off, and holding one in each hand he crept down the road. The sheriff didn't know whether his shots had taken effect, or whether John was setting an ambush for him, so he waited and listened. Then he suddenly realized that if a man stood in water six hours, the chances were pretty good his pistol wouldn't shoot, so he started down the road again.

John ran. *How* he ran! The sheriff matched him stride for stride, shooting and bellowing as he came. When he had fired six shots John knew his gun was empty, so he quit dodging from side to side and cut loose. The sheriff held his own. The chase led to one end of the mill, where a wide sluiceway crossed the path. The current was swift, it was about three feet deep, and spanned by one long plank. John hit it just right, and as he stepped off the far end the sheriff stepped on the end at his side. Always alert to an opportunity, the fleeing outlaw stopped, gave the plank one gigantic heave, and pitched the bridge and the sheriff into the racing current of the sluice. The last he heard of the sheriff that night was an outburst no writer would care to record!

Not knowing where the deputies were, John did not even dare pause for breath. He cut around the mill, heading for the main highway, and the woods on the far side.

The night watchman at the mill had heard the uproar, of course, and catching up a shot gun loaded with buckshot, he took a stand on a mound of sawdust and strained his eyes to see what was going on. John was headed right for him, and in the dark neither man could see the other. The outlaw was on him in a matter of seconds, and still not seeing the armed watchman, he crashed into him and sent him rolling end for end. John went to his knees, but was up and away like a streak. The watchman groped in the dark for his gun, raised it to his shoulder and fired both barrels at the spot where John had entered the brush. Flat on his face, the cagey fugitive had awaited the blast, and when the shot tore past he came to his feet and started running again. The two deputies were watching the other bank of the stream, so far away their excited shouts could barely be heard.

As he ran along, the outlaw considered his best course. He knew the sheriff would arm a huge posse and comb those woods, and he grinned in the dark as a bright idea came to him. The only place where the sheriff would never look for him would be right under his nose, so John trotted down the road toward Grand Rapids. His long hours of road work stood him in good stead now, and the exercise served to keep him warm in spite of his wet clothes. Alternating his pace between a trot and a fast walk, he reached the town long before daylight. Keeping to the shadows and the back alleys, he reached the rear of the saloon where he had been a bartender for a brief time. He worked a window up quietly, slipped in and closed it behind him. Picking his way between barrels and boxes, he reached the partition which separated the storeroom from the bar. He pinned his eye to a crack and saw that the saloon was empty, except for the bartender, who was leaning on the bar reading a newspaper. He put his lips to the crack and whispered, "Sam."

The startled bartender jumped and looked all around. John whispered, "In the storeroom. Keep quiet!"

Sam nodded, stretched, and looked around with elaborate casualness. The coast being clear, he opened the door into the storeroom and stepped inside. He recognized John in the dim light and started to laugh. Taking in the wet figure, Sam said, "I guess I don't need to tell you the sheriff is looking for you!"

John grinned back and said with a chuckle, "Oh, is *that* who I dumped in the sluiceway?"

The bartender shouted with glee, and John said, "Shut up, you fool! Do you want the whole town to know I'm here?"

"You aim to *stay* here," asked Sam, "right under the sheriff's nose?"

"You know of any safer place?" asked the outlaw, and the bartender had to stifle his mirth anew. "Boy," he said, "if we put *this* over, the whole North will be talking about it! Tell me what happened."

John said, "You tend bar, don't you? Well, when a cold, wet man comes into your joint, what does he get first?"

"Whiskey," said Sam, and went off to get it. He also brought a towel, a heavy coat, and a blanket. When John was dry and comfortable the two men sat where they could watch the saloon through the cracks in the boards of the dividing wall, and John regaled his friend with a circumstantial account of his escapades. Again and again he had to caution Sam to stifle his laughter, and they sat and talked until a late customer came in and Sam had to leave the storeroom for the bar.

John rolled up and slept on the floor, while the hue and cry went on miles from where he lay warm and dry. In the morning when Sam left he told his relief that Jack McWilliams was hiding in the warehouse, and the new man had to come in and hear the tale also. Delighted at a chance to help an old friend evade the law, he promised to keep a sharp eye out, and went back to work.

About ten o'clock that morning a crowd of men came in, all talking at once. The sheriff was convinced that John had made good his escape, and brought in his men. He was then busy warning the peace officers to the north that John was headed that way, after which he went back to arrest old Tom and charge him with aiding a fugitive to escape from the law.

In the crowd at the bar were many friends of the outlaw, and he stood with his eye to the crack watching them while they drank to his safe escape! The door opened and in came the watchman from the mill. He announced, "Everyone drink on me. I'm celebrating a narrow escape from a messy death!"

As the men crowded around demanding the details, the watchman said, "Well, sir, I was on duty at the mill last night, when I heard a lot of yelling and shooting down that old tote road. I says to myself, "Aha! The boys is running a moose. Here's where I get some fresh meat! So I grabbed my shot gun, loaded her up with buckshot and took a stand on a sawdust pile where I could watch the road. I no more than got set before the biggest moose you ever seen came snorting out of the woods, right at me. He charged me, hit me with his shoulder, and knocked me end fer end. In the dark I could feel him feeling around to stamp me, then he run off in the brush. I grabbed up my gun and give him both barrels, but he got away. I'll bet he had hams on him like an oak tree, I seen 'em! He must a weighed a ton! I'm lucky to be alive, I tell you!"

John almost choked, and the bartender *did!* He coughed and strangled and made noise enough so John could let out a little of the pressure. The boys were still exclaiming over his good fortune and narrow escape when someone said, "There goes the sheriff into the Court House, and he's got old Tom. The judge is waiting. Let's go and see what they give him. I'll bet it'll be ten years at least."

They filed out in a body, and crossed the road, or main street, and crowded into the courtroom. Sessions of courts on the frontier were apt to be informal, and they wasted very little time on this case.

The judge heard the sheriff recite his grievance against the darky, and then said to the prisoner, "Do you want a lawyer?"

"No, sir," said Tom, "I don't need no lawyer."

"How do you plead," asked the Court, "guilty or not guilty?"

"I pleads not guilty," said Tom.

The sheriff exploded, "Why, that's nonsense! He helped that man escape, and he'll go to jail for it."

"No I didn't," insisted Tom, "and no I won't. Judge, I wants a jury. And when the jury gits in the box, I gonna ask them three questions. First, I gonna say, 'Does you gennelmen know Jack McWilliams?' and they gonna say, 'Uh-huh!' Then I gonna say, 'He's a *bad* man!' and they gonna say, 'He sure is!' Then I gonna say, 'Gennelmen, if you was standing in a small, one-room, locked cabin facing the door and Jack McWilliams was standing behind you wid a baby cannon pushing in the middle of your back, *what would you do?*' Then I'm gonna say, 'Well, that's just what I done! Is you gennelmen gonna send me to jail for doing just what you would a done?' And that jury is gonna say, 'No, *sir,* we ain't!' So I don't need no lawyer, Judge. I just wants twelve men what knows Jack McWilliams and is fond of life!"

The judge leaned back and laughed with delight. When he could stop he wiped his eyes and pounded for order. The courtroom hilarity subsided, and the judge said, "Tom, you're right. No jury in this country would hold you. It would be a waste of time to try you. Case dismissed."

The disgusted sheriff cursed in hopeless rage, while the delighted crowd carried Tom over to the saloon to ply him with free drinks, while John listened to their recounts of how Tom outsmarted the law. He had done just as he had been told to do, and the affair ended as John thought it would.

He stayed hidden in his retreat for a week, fed by his friends and carefully concealed. Then he slipped out the window one night, and the woods swallowed him up again. So began a long siege of wandering, slinking from place to place, creeping like a hunted animal that goes in dread of its life, and getting lower and deeper in degradation as the weeks passed. His reputation was so bad that many a law officer saw and recognized him, and hastily looked the other way, not daring to attempt an arrest. Robbery and violence marked his trail, and on more than one occasion a saloon keeper would see him enter a saloon and take hasty action to prevent serious loss. Drawing the outlaw to one side, the tavern keeper would say, "Jack, you look like you are up against it. Here's twenty dollars to help you out. If you need more don't hesitate to come to me. Always glad to help an old friend!" Common courtesy would make it impossible for him to rob that establishment, and a proprietor could thus buy immunity.

One night John slept on the floor of a bar room, being broke and drifting. The next morning the marshal came in, shook him awake and said, "Did you ever hear of a fellow by the name of Jack McWilliams?"

John had a headache, a deep, dark, foul flavor in his mouth, a consuming thirst, and no money. He shook his head and said, "I don't remember. Maybe a drink would help."

The officer bought him a drink and repeated his query. John said, "I'm not sure. That drink is too lonesome to help much."

The marshal bought him a second and then a third drink, and said, "You look a lot like this Jack McWilliams the law is looking for."

John said, "Lots of good looking fellows in the world,

and I believe I am beginning to remember a little. Seems to me Jack is north of here."

The law said, "Have another drink, and if you can remember where he is, I'll give you five dollars to go tell him to do me a favor and stay away from this town. I don't want to tangle with him!" John took the five dollars, ambled out of town, and the marshal breathed a sigh of relief when the crisis was thus safely passed and diplomatically handled. And instead of questioning his courage, the sensible citizens all congratulated him on his wisdom and intelligence.

Word reached John that the political administration had changed in Grand Rapids, and a new sheriff occupied the office. The new incumbent was of a different kidney from his aggressive predecessor, and did not desire to tangle with the noted outlaw. He sent word via the grapevine that he would let bygones be bygones, and he would not bother John if the lawless man would observe a truce and commit no depredations in his jurisdiction. This was a break for John, who sadly needed a City of Refuge, and he drifted back to Grand Rapids and his old haunts.

Willing to take any sort of employment that would bring in an easy income, John hit the bottom and became a "runner" for a bawdy house! There is nothing lower in the estimation of sinful men than a commercialized panderer. The prodigal had reached the depths and became lower then the swine with whom he consorted. His dread reputation alone saved him from expressions of contempt, and the madame of the worst and largest brothel in the region boasted that the notorious Jack McWilliams was in her employ. Steeped in sin and violence, this poor prodigal lacked a sense of shame, and was quite content to wallow in the dregs of filth and lechery, sharing the wages of shame with the "girls" whose dubious charms he touted. There was no lower level he could reach—the prodigal had arrived.

# The Outlaw Reclaimed

# CHAPTER III

# The Outlaw Reclaimed

I once heard John Sornberger say, "The way of the transgressor *is* hard, and the last stages of the sinner's journey are the hardest and most degraded, because he is then on the bottom levels of vice and shame." He had a right to an opinion. He earned it the hard way. Among the rough and lewd men, who were his common companions, there was nothing reprehensible about his present position; all of the brothels had runners and the sad sisterhood all operated under the dubious "protection" of agents, who took a large share of the wages. When John had been working at this new racket for about a month, one of the women came to him with a business proposition. She said, "Jack, the man I work for is a dog and a thief. He robs me blind, but he is a mean devil, too handy with a knife in dark alleys, and everybody is afraid of him. I want to break loose from him, and I need help."

Always ready to aid anybody, John replied, "What do you want me to do? Shall I beat him up and throw him in the river? Want me to put a slug of lead in him and have the boys plant him? I can pick a fight with him and shoot him in self defense. Tell me how you want it handled."

The woman said, "No use you stirring up the local law and getting run out of town. That dirty so-and-so is afraid of only one man in this world, and that's you. So if you'd let me work for you, I'd give you the usual cut in my takings, and he'd have to leave me alone as long as I was your woman." John agreed to the arrangement, and added one more mark to his black score. Since he was kind to anyone or thing that was weaker than he, the woman had a far easier time of it, and praised him to the skies. So some of the other girls severed business relations with their managers and joined John's stable, and bad blood was aroused as a result.

One Monday morning, just before noon, all of the girls, the madame, and the agents were sitting around the breakfast table counting up their earnings and dividing their filthy wages of shame, when an argument started between one of the strumpets and the manager she had left when she went to work for John. The man had been drinking and was ugly, and was sitting just across the table from John. His anger boiled over, and he grabbed a fork from the table. Holding it like a throwing knife, he cast it with all of his strength at John, aiming for his right eye. Then he turned, leaped to his feet and dashed up the stairway which led to the upper story.

The fork struck just below the eye, and was imbedded in John's cheek. He surged to his feet, pulled the fork from his face with one hand as he drew his ready Colt with the other. The stairway was enclosed with pine boards so that John could not see his target, so he slowly and deliberately sprayed the stairs from the top down with six shots, hoping to catch his assailant with a well-placed bullet. His fifth and sixth shots both took effect, wounding the man severely, but fortunately not fatally. They heard the fleeing man stumble and fall, then start bouncing down as his slack form rolled from step to step.

The madame was out in the street shrieking for the law and the girls were all yelling for John to run and hide before the sheriff got there. One of his pals dashed in from the saloon, grabbed John and said, "I have a motor boat at the head of the dam. Come along and I'll run you up the river!"

John said, "You go first and get the motor started. I'll

run the other way to confuse the chase, circle around and come back to the boat."

The sheriff had heard the blast of gun fire, and was reasonably sure he knew who was to blame. He grabbed a rifle, called his three deputies, and headed for the scene of action. They arrived just in time to empty their guns at John as he disappeared around the corner. They paused to reload, and John gained enough headway so he could cut down another alley just as they came in sight and started firing again. For blocks they pursued him in what was destined to be his last brush with the law. I read a newspaper account of this affair which stated that more than forty shots were fired at the fleeing outlaw, none taking effect. But this last statement was not quite true. Just as John reached the bank of the river where his friend was waiting with the boat, a rifle ball hit him in the leg and he tumbled down the bank with a broken bone.

His pal pulled him in the boat and opened the throttle, and when the law arrived they were safely out of sight around a bend in the river. They kept going until they were within a mile of the homestead where the elder Sornberger lived, then they tied up in a heavy screen of willows and waited for darkness to fall. When black night had finally come, John's companion helped him to hobble that long, painful mile, using a rude branch for a crutch to support his broken leg. As they entered the clearing, they saw that the cabin was dark, so John knew that his father was in bed. He said to his helper, "There is a doctor in Grand Rapids named Brown. He will take care of the boys and keep his mouth shut if he gets paid. Take this fifty dollars and tell him a lad on the Hoot Owl Trail has a broken leg, and bring him here."

His friend signified his understanding, and hastened away. John opened the door and crept in. The prodigal was home! But flat on the floor, weak with pain, exposure, and loss of blood. His dad heard the noise of his entrance, lit a lamp and cried, "Who's there?"

The answer came back, "It's me, Father, your son John. I have a busted leg and I'm waiting for the doctor."

The grim old man towered above him and stared at him in somber silence for a long minute. Then his hand made a sweeping gesture toward the door as he said, "Get out! This is my home, and I'll harbor no outlaws in it!"

John said, "Father, I *can't* get out. My leg is broke. I'll be no trouble. Go back to bed and let me lie until the doctor comes, then I'll go."

"You'll go now!" was the implacable reply. Putting his lamp on the table, the gaunt, white-haired old man seized his outlaw son by the coat collar, dragged him to the open door and heaved him out into the night. The pain and the movement of his broken bone proved too much, and John passed out.

When he revived some time later, he lay and thought over his plight. He remembered an old, disused root cellar near the edge of the clearing, and he painfully dragged himself to it. He rested on the ground outside the cellar until he heard his friend and the doctor steal into the clearing, and then called them to his side by a low whistle. They carried him inside the damp root cellar, and there by the light of a kerosene lantern they dressed his wound and set his leg. The doctor said he'd come back in a few days and look at it again, and in the meantime he was just to lie quiet. They left him some food, a bottle of whiskey, the lantern and a can of kerosene, and slipped away.

Three times in the next two weeks posses came and went, but the old root cellar had been abandoned for so long it was completely forgotten, and so escaped notice. When the sheriff arrived on his first search, Mr. Sornberger made no attempt at evasion. "Yes," he replied to the sheriff's query. "The man you want was here. He tried to take refuge in my house and I cast him out into the night!" Looking into the fierce eyes of the old man the sheriff shivered and never doubted his word. So, when the father said he had not seen John since that first night, the chase went off in another direction and quiet settled down in the clearing.

John's friend kept him supplied with food and drink, and the doctor made an occasional trip in the night, all of which the hidden man paid for, and paid dearly. When the splints were taken off his leg, the doctor expressed satisfaction at his condition, and told him he could move on as soon as his leg got used to bearing his weight. Another week he waited, lying low all day and exercising his leg at night, then he took council with his friend as to which way he should head. Bad news surrounded him at every point of the compass. The country to the south was still being combed by possés, and to the east and the west a cordon of peace officers were on the alert. All of the northern counties were being watched, and John decided that Canada offered the only safe haven, if he could reach it.

By trails that were seldom used he reached Brainerd, worn to a shadow. He robbed a store there and got some supplies, then travelled until he reached the Black Duck Camp. There a friendly cook hid him for a week while he rested and got his strength back, when he again went on the dodge, arriving at Walker. Once again he loaded his pack and got fresh ammunition, and was out again before dawn. Struggling on, he got within a few miles of Cass Lake and played out. A day and a night he rested in an open field like a beast of the wild, then went into Cass Lake and asked for a job in the camp. The labor boss was a new man in that section and had never seen the noted outlaw, and hands were as scarce as hens' teeth. He said, "I need a cook. Can you cook?" John knew that the first place the law would look for him would be in the kitchen, so he said, "I never cooked a meal in my life."

"Too bad," the boss answered. "The only other thing

I have is a job swamping—away out in the deep woods of the back country. It's so far out nobody else will take it. It pays twenty-two dollars a month. Do you want it?"

John did! In the early days in the North woods, the brush was the ultimate refuge of every hunted man. In some of the distant camps, if a law officer paid a visit, a full third of the crew disappeared in the brush until he was safely away. Twenty-two dollars a month was awfully small change to a man who had tossed away fortunes, but a hideout was more important than wealth, so the woods swallowed him once again, and toil claimed him.

This was a mercy, for he was at the end of his rope. Now, cut off from booze and laboring in the open air, eating regularly and sleeping like a log, he gained his strength and health back and began to feel like his old self again. Nobody in the camp bothered him, and the few who recognized him just winked as they passed him, and kept their mouths shut. So time drifted past for almost five months, and the chase for Jack McWilliams was no longer pressed. John figured that in another two months he could hit the road again.

But fate had it planned otherwise. He was doomed to be captured at last. For one Sunday, as the men were eating dinner, the door was kicked open and a huge frame filled the opening. One of the men hollered, "Hey! It's the Sky Pilot!" and a score of voices shouted, "Hullo, Frank, how did *you* ever get away back in here?"

Laughing and returning the good-natured banter, Frank Higgins entered and sat down, throwing his pack in the corner as he entered. While he was filling his plate with food, John was studying him. He had often heard of the famous lumberjack evangelist, but had never seen or heard him before. He always insisted that "all preachers were just windbags," and classified Higgins with the others. He was surprised at the kindly humor of the homely, attractive face, and stared with appreciation and envy at

116

the tremendous shoulders, so wide they made their owner look square. John was sitting by the door, and felt he could cut and run if the visitor recognized him. He took it for granted that any preacher would inform the law if he saw a wanted man. But Higgins paid no attention to him, and he was careful to sit still and not be conspicuous. After eating, the men returned to the bunkhouse where such meetings were customarily held. Frank pulled a Bible out of his pocket and said, "Boys, I've come to have a service with you."

John was trapped and did not dare make a break, fearing to excite curiosity.

He sat with a sneer on his face as the rude men blended their voices in a terrible lack of harmony and complete indifference to time and tune, while Frank led them in a few old hymns. His eyes were the only ones not closed with reverence when the Sky Pilot prayed, and he was still sneering when Frank opened the Bible. The Sky Pilot had sensed his opposition and malice by this time, and had a shrewd eye on him. To himself the preacher said, "That's one of the toughest looking birds I ever laid eyes on. If I had a dollar and he was around, I'd stay out of dark alleys."

He began his sermon by saying, "Boys, I want to tell you today about a parable Jesus told to a crowd that was even rougher than you, and which is known as the "Story of the Prodigal Son." It's two thousand years old, but the story is as true as though it had been written yesterday." With this opening Frank went on in his simple, forcefully clear and logical style to portray the great and changeless drama which the reader so well knows. His voice was rich and powerful, and its deep melody entranced the listeners.

He sketched the peace and happiness of the home where a man of means dwelt with his two sons. He told of the love of that family circle, and the comfort and security they all showed. Skillfully he made every man in the room

Falling Timber

Skidding Logs to the Landing

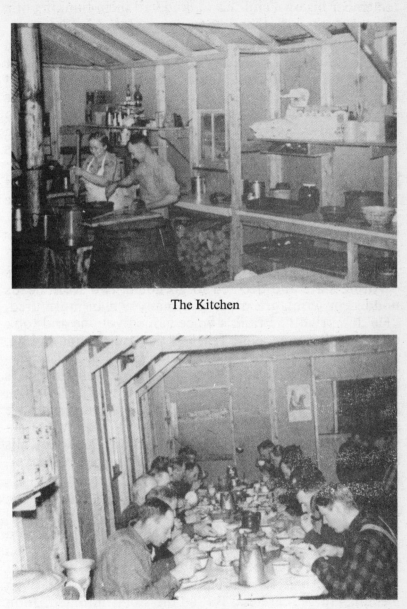

The Kitchen

The Dining Room

remember his own childhood, and had them thinking of a warm hearth, a mother's hopes, and a father's care.

Then he sketched the wild longings of the younger son for adventure and pleasure, and made every man feel the lust for living that drove the lad away from the safety of home into the far country. His description of the pleasures of indulgence was not fanciful. He painted the common sins of the lumberjack's experience, and made every man think ruefully that somebody had sketched the listener's portrait in the spoken words. And when he came to the bitter downfall of a lad who had ridden high and rolled with the best, every man there knew from sad experience just how the culprit felt! To them it was a logical end, for their drunken orgies had often left them fit company for swine, and unsuited to any other or higher circles of life.

When the preacher told how the boy awakened to his destitute state and decided to go home, two score heads nodded in wise agreement and many a man murmured, "He done right!" Frank's voice gained volume and took on a bell-like tone as he reached the triumphant ending, and when he cried out the father's words of welcome—"This my son was dead and is alive again, was lost and is found," the listening jacks almost shouted with him. Then in a few words he applied the story to all men who are separated from God, and who live in the wallows of sin when they could be in the Father's family and in His sheltering love. When he finished with a word of prayer, he excused himself and hurried outside.

He had been watching John from the start of the service, although the outlaw had tried to keep his face down and shaded. Frank had seen the sneer on his lips and the hatred in his eyes as the service started, and had been keeping a wary eye on what might prove to be a source of trouble. He had seen too many attempts to break up meetings to get careless. But as the story unfolded, John began to see himself in the picture, and for the first time in many years he thought of his childhood home. He remembered his mother—dead when he was just beginning to really know her, and the kindly foster parents who had loved him. He even remembered the dog he had played with and loved. Face after face flashed across the screen of his memory. When the prodigal landed in the depths, broke, his fine raiment gone and swine for companions, a bitter smile crossed his lips and he nodded in agreement with the justice of the result. He had lived every word of that story!

Frank had noticed the dawning interest wipe the black scowl from John's brow, and he had been preaching straight at the desperate man. He was delighted to see the manifest interest grow deeper and deeper, and so was amazed at John's action when he told of the prodigal's homecoming. Instead of being pleased, as the others so evidently were, John suddenly jumped to his feet and fled cursing from the room. The door banged behind him and he was gone from sight.

So as soon as he could, Frank went out in search of him. He found John out behind the cook house, his face still dark with anger.

The huge preacher, who feared nothing on this earth, went up to the angry man and asked, "What was the matter, friend? Didn't you like that story?"

With a bitter oath John said he did not!

"Don't you believe," asked Frank, "that the prodigal came to a bad end?"

"Oh, that part's all right," said John, "as far as that goes. I've slept with pigs myself and et plenty of husks in my day. He got just what was coming to him. So did I, and I ain't whining. But that soft slop about his old man taking him in is a lot of hogwash. I know better, Mister! I went home when even the pigs wouldn't have me. I was sick, helpless, all in. I lay on the floor of my father's house and asked for help. You know what *my* old man did? He took me by the neck, drug me to the door, and throwed me out into the night like a dog! So I don't *believe* that stuff about the calf and the robe and the ring. I know better!''

The bitterness of that outburst would have appalled a lesser man, but Higgins knew life in the raw, and stood his grounds. "I see what you mean," he said, "but you went to the wrong father. You should have gone to the Other One first."

John was puzzled, and said, "I only have one father, and I told you what *he* did to me."

Subtly Frank drew the outlaw into a discussion: "Was he a religious man?"

"I'll say he was. Read the Bible all the time."

"Was he a hypocrite, who preached one thing and practised another?"

"Not at all. He was honest as the day and as straight as a string."

"Did he know some of the devilment you had been into, dragging his name in the dirt, maybe, and breaking his heart with wild living?"

"Yeah, he knew my record, all right. Why do you ask?"

"Because, I'd like a straight answer to a plain question: Knowing your father's principles, and remembering how you have lived, can your father be blamed for kicking you out?"

For long minutes there was silence as the hunted man recalled the path he had pursued, and the sorrow and pain he must have caused his godly dad. Then in a voice deep with conviction he said, "*My old man done just right!*"

Frank smiled and said, "There is always hope for a man who doesn't try to kid himself. Now, if you had gone to your *other* Father first, the Father who is in Heaven, and had gotten right with Him you would have had a happier homecoming. Friend, I don't know who you are nor what you have done, but God has promised "whosoever cometh unto me I will in no wise cast out." He gave His Son Jesus Christ to die for your sins, and if you put your life in His keeping He will straighten out all the crooked trails and make you fit to go home."

"Not me," said John, "I'm too low and vile for even God to do anything with."

The preacher stopped him with a gesture and said, "Read these words: 'If we walk in the light as He is in the light, we have fellowship one with another, and the blood of Jesus Christ, God's Son, cleanseth us from all sin.' Now God says 'all.' He doesn't mean half or nearly all, and if you were Judas or the devil's own partner, God could save you."

"What is this light you're talking about, the which we got to walk in?" asked John.

The preacher answered, "Jesus said, 'I am the light of the world. He that followeth after me shall not walk in darkness, but shall have the light of life.' Friend, you believe that Jesus was the Son of God, don't you?"

John said, "I ain't so ignorant as to doubt that."

Higgins pressed him closer, "And God has promised in these words, 'If thou shalt confess with thy mouth Jesus as Lord, and hast believed in thy heart that God has raised him from the dead, thou shalt be saved.' To be saved means to have all your sins pardoned, to have a new life started for you to live all over again, and the help of God to get free from all that is wicked and unclean. *Are you a sinner? Do you want salvation?*"

John fell on his face as though he had been hit with a maul. All of his past sin and violence rose up before him to condemn him, and he wept like a child. Pain, wounds, bullets, and broken bones had never been able to dampen his cheeks, but the thought of mercy and help from Heaven broke his hard spirit. In agony he cried out to God, "Save me for Jesus' sake," and as though a voice shouted in his ear he heard the promise, "I *have* heard you, and saved you, for Jesus' sake!" All of his life he insisted that God spoke to him then, and who can say that it was not so? Frank was on his knees praying, when John suddenly grew limp and still. In some concern the Sky Pilot reached out a hand and touched him, and said, "Friend, are you all right?"

"Yes," John answered, "I *am* all right. God has saved me for Jesus' sake, and I'll never go back on Him!"

Higgins drew John to his feet and said, "There are two mighty happy men in this camp. You and me. I am glad God sent me this way. What is your name?"

It was the first test. John started to lie by force of habit, then he looked Frank in the eye and said, "Did you ever hear of Jack McWilliams?"

The Sky Pilot was almost too stunned to grasp it for a minute, then he cried, "Are *you* Jack McWilliams?"

John nodded and said, "Does that make any difference?"

The huge preacher threw back his head and shouted, "Hallelujah!" and grabbed Jack and hugged him to his heart, with tears of joy streaming down his own broad face. Over and over he shouted, "Praise God! Praise God! Praise God!" until the crew came running to see what had happened. Frank said, "Boys, this is the greatest conversion since Paul the Apostle!" That meant nothing to John, who thought that Paul was probably a lumberjack who worked in the region!

All afternoon Frank talked with John and prayed with him, and John said, "What shall I do about all of those indictments and warrants standing out against me? Don't you think I had better go to Bemidji and give myself up, and take my medicine?"

After some thought, Frank counseled against the idea, saying, "Let's see what we can work out. I'll be pulling out in the morning, and you stay here until you hear from me."

John was too happy to eat any supper, and he sat and

read the Bible Frank had given him until he could keep his eyes open no longer. Then he knelt by the side of his bunk and prayed for the first time since he was a small boy, and slept in peace. The next morning at the breakfast table he got up and made a speech. He said, "Boys, yesterday I got converted. I took Jesus as my Saviour and now I aim to live for God if I hang for it. I been foul-mouthed and dirty in my speech. I'll never take the name of God in vain again. Don't ever offer me a drink. I'm done with liquor, and I'll never draw a gun on a fellow man, even in self defense. As far as I can I'll pay back what I have stole, and I am going to serve God any way I can."

Some of the men marveled, some made bets that he'd be drunk next pay day, and a few said he had gone crazy! But things began to break for John in a hurry. Two days after his conversion it began to snow, and the foreman told the men to lay off for the day, as it was the first snow of the season and it had caught them unprepared. There was some complaining, as lumberjacks are supposed to work in spite of the weather, and they did not like to lose pay for idle days. But in the middle of the afternoon Frank Higgins came back, bringing with him a man named Ward, who was the owner of the timber and who operated a huge saw mill. Frank called the idle men together for a meeting in the camp, and they were pleased as always to have him preach to them. When the service ended, John started out with the other men, and Higgins met him outside the door. He shook hands with the outlaw and asked, "How are you making it?"

"Just fine," John said, "I've never been so happy in all of my life. I feel a thousand pounds lighter! I want to jump around and holler, and I'm spending every minute I can reading the Bible you gave me."

The Sky Pilot was elated, and asked, "What are your plans?"

John replied, "I've been thinking a lot about that. I still

think I ought to give myself up and take what's coming to me."

But the preacher said, "Not yet. There is always time for that. I'm working on a plan and I want you to lay low until I tell you how it comes out. Will you promise me to do nothing until I talk with you?"

"Sure," said John, "I promise, but suppose the law catches up with me?"

"Then we will have to let it take its couse," Higgins said, "and do what we can under the circumstances. But they haven't got you yet, so let's worry about that when it happens."

He called Mr. Ward over to them and said, "Mr. Ward, this is Jack McWilliams. I want you to meet him."

The owner's eyes stuck out like buttons as he said, "The famous outlaw?"

"Yes," Higgins agreed, "but two days ago a miracle happened, and Jack was converted. Now he's saved and he is going to live for the Lord."

"Is that right?" Ward demanded.

"*Yes*, sir!" Jack almost shouted. "I've been on the dodge for years, but Jesus Christ captured me, and I'm his prisoner now."

"Man alive!" cried the excited owner, "You can't stay *here*! They'll get you sure! If you are a Christian now, I want to help you and see that you get a fair chance. I'll tell you what you had better do. I am opening a new camp forty miles in, and the law will never get in there. I'll make you assistant foreman and send you in where you'll be safer for a while. The pay is $85 a month. Is that all right?"

So John found another friend, got a raise of almost four hundred percent, and was hustled to a place of refuge while his friends went to work in his behalf. Higgins talked to Sheriff Bailey at Bemidji, told him Jack McWilliams was converted, and asked him to get the indictments suppressed. But the sheriff had not forgotten the barrage of rude humor he had faced when Jack had gotten away from him, and he said, "I'll put that bird in the penitentiary if I die doing it!" The other peace officers all felt the same way, and the Sky Pilot could get no help or sympathy from the authorities.

For one thing, none of them believed John had been really converted. Sheriff Bailey stated flatly, "I know that fellow, and he is bad clear through. There are some things even God can't do, and making a Christian and an honest man out of that hardened law breaker is one of those things." But John was quietly giving proof of the reality of his conversion. The cook in the new camp became sick, and John nursed him and took over his duties. The men ate better meals than any they had ever tasted before, and they were delighted. When Sunday came, John gathered the crew together, read the Bible to them, had prayer, and gave his testimony again. This time the men believed him, and after the service the jacks called a meeting. The leaders served warning that anyone who offered John a drink would be ducked in the river and run out of camp! They said he was going to have a chance to live a Christian life if they could possibly give it to him.

Two months later Frank Higgins showed up, and took John off to a neighboring camp to help in a service, and to give his testimony. He began the service saying, "I wouldn't trust any other crowd of men in the world with this secret, but you boys are all lumberjacks, and not one of you would ever turn one of your own gang over to the law. So I'm going to tell you that this man here is Jack McWilliams, the hated outlaw."

There was a surge of excitement as the boys craned their necks and stood up in the rear of the crowd trying to get a better look at the most notorious man in their world. Frank said, "What all the forces of the law could not do,

God did. He laid Jack by the heels. He was converted, and I'm going to ask him to tell you how it happened."

John rose to his feet, opened his Bible, and read again the story of the Prodigal Son. Then he closed the Book and began, "*I* am that prodigal son." Simply but forcefully he reviewed his career, sparing himself in no particular. He gave the men details of his rise to fame, and said that he had not been defeated by the famed Australian champion, but by a combination of bad booze, worse women, and John Sornberger! He convinced the listeners that when it came to "riotous living" he was an authority, and told how he hit the toboggan slide of sin when he left the prize ring. The men shivered with sympathy when he described cold nights spent in the wet brush, not daring to sleep with the hounds of the law searching the woods all about him. In graphic words he made them feel the terror and despair of the hunted thing, and they shouted with appreciative mirth when he told how he bamboozled the law and left the marshal locked up in his own jail. Then in words which came from his heart he described his conversion, and was not ashamed of the tears which stained his cheeks as he gave God praise and gratitude for his salvation.

The Sky Pilot listened with delighted wonder, saying to himself, "Why, the man is an orator! What a preacher he would make!" Then a few minutes later he thought, "Why not? God can make the crooked ways straight, and he may have saved John Sornberger for a purpose, just as he did Saul of Tarsus." And in a silent but fervent prayer, Frank Higgins claimed John Sornberger as an ally and an aid, and God wonderfully answered his petition in the days that came.

For four months Frank led John around from camp to camp, wherever they were remote enough from the reach of the law, and then he told John he had business in the Twin Cities and would be gone for some time. He asked his new convert to take charge of the meetings in the camps on Sundays while he was away, and John gladly consented. The owner, Ward, was a staunch Presbyterian, who backed the Sky Pilot to the limit, the foreman was a devout Catholic of liberal and broad views on denominational questions, and nobody cared how much John neglected the work he was paid for. So he visited the sick, helped the men write letters, preached and testified, and studied his Bible by the hour, until one day Mr. Ward drove into camp and handed John a telegram from Frank Higgins which read:

"I am in a jam in St. Paul trying to help a friend. Will you come at once and help me?"

Frank.

In less than thirty minutes John had his pack ready, and rode out with Ward. When he reached the railroad he bought a ticket and rode to St. Paul. He was quite safe. No one would recognize in him the hunted man. His eyes were clear and bright, he was sturdy with health, and six months of black growth covered his face. His hair was almost as long as an Indian's so he looked like any one of ten thousand jacks coming out of the woods after a six months' stretch of work. He had four hundred dollars in his pocket and felt like he owned the world.

Frank met him at the train and said, "Don't ask any questions right now, but do as I tell you and I'll explain later. You look wild enough to scare yourself! Go get a haircut, a shave, a massage, a bath, and a good suit of clothes and come to my hotel. Do you need any money?"

John assured his friend that he was well-heeled, and went to get refurbished. He got what the boys called "the works" at the barber shop, bought some new clothes, and even got a handkerchief with some perfume on it to finish up the job. Frank was delighted with his civilized appearance, and asked him if he had ever been in St. Paul. John said he had been there when he was in the ring, but didn't know much about the city. The wily Higgins said,

"Well, we are going over there now and get in touch with some pretty important people, and see if they can help this friend of mine. You follow my lead and answer any questions they ask you."

When they were near the Capitol, Frank said, "John, here is where we make our first call. Stick close to me and do just as I tell you." They entered the Capitol, went down a long hall, and entered a waiting room where two score people were waiting. Frank went up to a secretary seated at a desk and said, "Mr. Day, this is the man we were talking about." The secretary replied, "Hullo, Higgins, the governor is expecting you, you are to walk right in. He said to give you precedence over anyone else who might be waiting."

It was not until they were in the governor's office that John knew what had happened. He felt trapped, and looked around for a way out, but all the doors were closed, the windows were too high to reach, and he saw that he was unable to either fight or run. He trusted Higgins, and knew that if he was delivering a friend to the law, it was the best thing to do.

Governor Johnson stood to his feet and surveyed John with frank curiosity. He smiled and said, "Mr. Sornberger, or Jack McWilliams, I am frankly surprised. From the reports which have flooded my office I looked to see a shaggy, huge, desperado. I see instead a man who appears to be a gentleman. What brought you to such a sorry state that half of the sheriffs of this state are calling for your blood?"

John said, "I am afraid they have exaggerated my character and my deeds. And if you had any sheriffs worth shooting—"

"Shut up!" the governor said sternly. "As long as you try to justify yourself you are on dangerous ground! Do you deny that you are a bad man, a scamp, a scoundrel who richly deserves jail?"

"No, sir, Governor!" John answered earnestly, "I do *not* deny that. I deserve worse than jail. I ought to be in Hell! But Jesus came to my rescue. God has saved me, and I'm ready to go to jail if you say so. I reckon I can preach in jail as well as I can in the woods!"

The governor smiled with pleasure, put his arm around the outlaw and said, "John, I feel happy and honored to know you. Not because of what you were, but because of what you have become. Never go back on the God who has done so much for all of us in and through the cross of His Son!" Then turning to the Sky Pilot, he said, "Mr. Higgins, I am convinced. This man is really converted. Nothing but the power of God Almighty can put before our happy eyes a man like this, made over from the man he was. I will be misunderstood, I will be condemned, I will be criticized for this, but I have a duty as a Christian which means more than my political career. I am going to give this man a full and complete pardon, and leave him free to serve our blessed Saviour."

Governor Johnson stepped to his desk, wrote and signed a full pardon for John Sornberger, alias Jack McWilliams, and John was a free man. He wept with joy, and the governor, deeply moved, put one arm around Frank and the other around John, and said, "Boys, let us pray!" And the governor of the state knelt in his office, with his arms around the noted Sky Pilot, and the most dreaded outlaw of the realm, and committed them both to the Grace of God. Rising to their feet the governor said, "Write to me, John, and come and see me often. I'll be interested in knowing how you get along, and in hearing about your career as a preacher." John promised, and they left the executive's office.

When they got outside, John suddenly asked, "Who is this friend of yours I was supposed to help?"

Frank threw his head back and bellowed with laughter as he replied, "Oh, he's all right now, the *governor* took care of *him*!'' John joined in his friend's mirth and they went merrily on their way.

Governor Johnson was right. A storm of protest *did* go up over the governor's act. Every sheriff and marshal in the state objected to the pardoning of a man who had forty-two indictments and warrants out against him, and some of the most influential politicians called on the governor to make an official protest. But the executive refused to be moved. He said, ''My friends, I looked into the eyes and the heart of a man who was rescued from Hell by our Lord Jesus, and I do not intend to thrust him back in again! A notable miracle was wrought by God's grace when John Sornberger was saved—as much a miracle as when Lazarus was raised from the dead. I do have a duty to the people of Minnesota, but above and before that is my duty to God. I counted the cost before I pardoned this man. I promised him my help, and I shall stick to him if it costs me my office and my career. And I will prophesy that the time will come when the whole state will congratulate me for so doing!'' The governor was right. His friends later boasted of his wisdom and foresight in restoring citizenship to a famed outlaw, and helping him to set his feet upon a straight path.

When John was pardoned, one of the angriest men in the entire state was Sheriff Bailey of Bemidji. In his wrath he stated publicly: ''Pardon or no pardon, if he dares show his face in my jurisdiction I'll shoot him on sight!'' In the meantime, John was itinerating from camp to camp at his own expense, preaching and giving his testimony. He left a blaze of interest behind him, and his favorite sermon was on the theme, ''The Outlaw Reclaimed.'' Word reached him that Sheriff Bailey was still gunning for him, so, characteristically, John headed for Bemidji! He had two jobs to take care of over there, and he was never one to shirk danger or duty. To his dying day he never changed in one trait: he would fight at the drop of a hat if he thought the occasion called for it. In defence of himself, his religion, the under dog, or a friend, John's fists were always cocked and ready to explode.

When he pulled into Bemidji he rounded up a half dozen old friends and took them along to "see the fun." He walked into the sheriff's office, where the peace officer was sitting at his desk. John opened friendly negotiations with the diplomatic remark, "I hear you are going to shoot me on sight. Well, take a look, pull your gun, and start shooting!"

The sheriff flew into a rage, and his efforts to suppress it turned him as red as a turkey's wattle. He was afraid to make a move with John just across the desk and planted firmly on his feet, so he stalled for time by saying, "What would *you* do if I *did* pull my gun?"

Without raising his voice John promised, "I'd take it from you and wind it around your neck!"

The sheriff was pretty sure he spoke the truth, so he changed the subject by saying, "I see you brought your gang with you. Is that why you feel so brave?"

John spit on the floor in contempt, and said, "Mister, you are yellow clear through. The only time you ever dared come close to me was when you sneaked up in the dark behind me in your sock feet. You stuck a gun in my back because you were afraid to see my face. I brought these boys along to make sure you don't shoot me in the back when I am leaving. The governor pardoned me. Your warrants are no good, and you wouldn't have the nerve to serve them if they were. Since I got a pardon I am a citizen again, but Mister, I don't believe I am ever going to vote for you!" Then he turned on his heel and walked out, followed by his laughing pals.

One of them said, "John, when I saw you last, if you pulled a stunt like that, I'd have said, 'I'll buy the drinks.' But I don't guess you buy whiskey for a preacher. What does a man say in them conditions?"

John laughed and replied, "He says, 'Preacher, when

you hold a service tomorrow night,' (like I am going to in Peterson's old warehouse) 'I'll be there to hear you preach, and I'll bring some of the boys with me.' That's the best thing any of my old friends can do to please me."

"It's a bet," was the reply. "I'll have the whole crew there if I have to lay them out and drag them in one at a time."

Leaving the crowd, John went about his other errand. As you may remember, he had a common law wife living in Bemidji, and she had three children of whom John was presumably the father. He felt he owed a duty there, and went to see her. She welcomed him in by saying, "What's this I hear about you being a Christian, and becoming a preacher? Is it some sort of a hurrah you are working on the law?"

"No," John said. "It's real. I have been saved, and now I aim to live for God. And since I am a Christian I came to make you a proposition. I feel obligated to you because of the past, and if you will accept Christ and give up booze and the old life, I'll marry you and make a home for you, and support the three children."

The woman laughed in his face. "*That* I'll never do," she declared. "I wouldn't be a hymn-singing preacher's wife if I died for not being! As for the kids, how do *you* know who is their father? I don't know that myself! I'll take care of my own life—just say 'good-bye' and beat it!" So John turned away, unable to make any restitution for that sad chapter, but feeling he had done his best.

Turning back to Grand Rapids, still following his back trails and testifying to a changed life, John walked into the office of the sheriff who had harried him and pursued him for years, and now re-elected and back in office after a lapse of one term. He saw John coming and went to meet him with his hand outstretched and a smile on his face. He said, "Jack, when I heard about your pardon I said, 'Thank God, now I can sleep nights and not get grey-headed trying to out-smart a buzzard that is smarter than me!' I always had a sneaking liking for you, and boy! I sure wish you luck!''

Jack shook hands with his old-time enemy and said, "Sam, you are the only law man I ever feared. When I heard you was on my tail I tucked it in between my legs and ran for Canada! I always admired your guts. I like a brave man, and you are the only sheriff who tried to take me face to face. I'd like to be friends with you!" And until the hour John conducted the funeral service for the noted officer, they were closer than brothers.

It was with some doubt as to his welcome that John then sought his father's cabin on the homestead. He had written to tell his dad of his conversion and of the pardon issued by the governor, but knew the implacable memory of the stern old man. When he opened the door and went in, his father was packing an old telescope bag. John said, "Hullo, Father!" His dad looked at him a long, long minute. He took in the clear eyes, unclouded by drink. He saw the firm and healthy looking cheeks, the assurance of the man who knows he is clean and in good condition. He nodded as though confirming to himself his impressions, thrust out his hand, and said, "Hullo." That's all there was to it, either then or later. No fatted calf or silken robe, no golden ring and wild rejoicing; just a quiet acceptance of a son back into his birthright and the right to use his father's name. Word spread quickly that John was there, and the neighbors began to gather. They asked John if he was going to preach while there. Quick, as always, to grasp an opening, he said he intended to have an open air meeting in the clearing that night. They left, promising to bring all of their friends to hear the ex-outlaw's sermon.

John had a native knack for the spectacular and the dramatic, and his years in the ring had developed him as a capable showman. So when the crowd gathered, he called them together at the edge of the clearing, using the old root cellar as a pulpit! He preached on "Me, the Prodigal Son" and told of his reception when he came seeking refuge wounded and broken. The neighbors chuckled with delight when the preacher told how he had lain in that very spot for weeks while the law combed the region for him, and the drama of the changed situation stirred them all. In the course of his sermon, John stated, "I don't have to tell you that I was a wicked man and a desperate sinner. You know what I was, but none of you, my old neighbors, can brag very much about being righteous. In this crowd of not over two hundred people there ain't a man except my father that ain't been drunk with me. We are *all* prodigals—the only difference being that I sorrowed for my sin, gave it all up, took Jesus for my Savior and turned to God. And anyone of you that desires a better life can have it. The door into God's house is Jesus, who said, 'I am the door, by me if any man enter in he shall be saved'." And when he pressed the claims of Christ upon them in the plain and frank terms which marked his preaching from the start of his career, he had the joy and satisfaction of seeing several of his old companions in sin and violence turn to Christ and salvation. None could doubt that a miracle had happened in *his* life, they knew him "before and after" as several of them stated.

After the meeting, when John and his dad were alone, the old man said, "I was packing to leave when you came in, and I have to start out tomorrow. I have a good job up at Bigfork. When you come up that way look me up, will you?" John promised, and slept that night, the first time in many bitter years, a welcome guest in his father's house.

After his dad had pulled out, John stayed around Grand Rapids for about a week. Then a man came seeking him to offer him a good job. It was the custom then for contractors to undertake the feeding of laborers in camps, construction jobs, and on railroad building projects. Such boarding masters had rolling equipment which they moved from place to place as the jobs changed. It was an important undertaking, as woodsmen would put up with any hardship and suffer the most rigid conditions if they were well fed. They wanted huge meals of food that would stick to their ribs, and it had to be well and tastefully cooked. The most important man in any camp was the cook. He could keep the men cheerful and contented or he could start civil war at any time.

Mr. Alberts had several such boarding contracts, and he had a difficult time keeping his cooks in line. They would drink and neglect their work, and, if he tried to fire one of them, the belligerent kitchen despot would take a butcher knife or cleaver and run the boss right out of camp! Alberts needed a "traveling cook" to boss his outfits, one who could handle bad men, and in a pinch take over the kitchen and feed hungry crews. He offered John the job, stating his willingness to pay $175 a month to get him in his employ.

John jumped at the chance, because it would keep him traveling from camp to camp, and give him a grand chance to preach to large numbers of men. So Mr. Alberts wrote out his credentials and gave him his first assignment. He said, "I have an outfit up near Cass Lake that is dynamite. The cook has been drunk a week, and the men are wild enough to lynch him. Go up there and fire him, and stayed on the job feeding the men until I send up another cook to take over."

The new boss cook started thirty minutes later. When he arrived at Cass Lake the evening meal had just been finished, and the sullen crew was standing around cursing the cook, the company, the contractor and everybody concerned. John strode into camp, threw down his pack and bellowed for attention. The curious men gathered around the newcomer, who said, "Boys, I'm John Sornberger, the ex-outlaw who used to be called Jack McWilliams. I have come to fire the cook and take over and feed you boys. Come along and watch me do it!"

With a whoop of delight the men followed their new champion, and clustered around the screened cook shack to see the show. John stepped inside the door, spotted the cook and said, "You're fired! Pack your knapsack, roll your blankets and get out of camp in thirty minutes."

The cook was full of alcoholic courage, and said, "And if I don't?"

John said, "Then I'll throw you out feet first!"

The cook grabbed a butcher knife and ran at the interloper. This was old stuff to John. He just stood until the cook was on him, then he shifted, grabbed the arm that held the knife and gave it a wrench. The cook squawked and dropped the knife. John hit him just once, and the cook folded into oblivion. Then he turned to the crew and said, "Throw this drunken food spoiler out of my kitchen. I got work to do if you boys are going to eat a decent breakfast in the morning." The men cheered and laughed, and the limp form of the cook was taken by more or less kindly hands and dumped in the creek, where the cold water revived him. A half hour later he left, carrying his pack and a sore jaw. Friday and Saturday the men ate meals fit for a king, and a huge contentment filled their world. But at the breakfast table Sunday morning the new cook came in and made a sad announcement. He stood on a bench and said, "Boys, I'm sorry to leave you, but you see I am a preacher, not a cook. I can't be happy without I am preaching, so I'm pulling out in the morning and going back where I can preach."

There was a stunned silence for a minute, then some jack got a bright idea and hollered, "What's the matter with staying right here and preaching to *us?* We need it, don't we, boys?"

A roar of agreement went up from the men, and with a straight face the wily cook said, "Well, if you want it that way, I guess I can do so. Tell you what you do: As soon as the lunch dishes are done, we'll have a meeting in the dining hall. If you like my preaching, I'll stay until the new cook comes to take over the job, and I won't leave then unless he's a good one.'' The crowd at the afternoon meeting set an attendance record of one hundred per cent; the men were not going to lose their cook if they could help it! John was a natural orator, a dramatic speaker who enacted his ideas as he talked, and the men were thrilled with his message. They asked for another sermon that night, and needless to say they got it. John stayed for three weeks before his relief came, bringing orders for John to go to Black Lake and clean up another mess there. And every night of that three weeks he held a service or conducted a Bible Class, with the result that many of the crew found Christ and peace, and were in the Kingdom of God when the time came for John to leave them. When he walked out of camp, fifty men went with him for the first few miles, and rough, rude, and lusty as they were, they were not ashamed of their wet eyes as they turned back after watching their preacher out of sight.

John had found himself and his work. He left that camp knowing how he was to serve God. He determined to walk in the footsteps of his idol, Frank Higgins, to be a Sky Pilot to the boys in the woods. Destined to tour the great centers of America and address multitudes, he always returned to his North woods and the people and work he loved. Like Higgins, he also was to die in the harness, but a long, hard road stretched ahead of him before he laid aside his pack sack and his Bible for the Better Land. Although he did not know it then, his feet were on a shining trail, and the joy and pleasure which came to him thereafter grew out of a work done for God in the hearts of needy fellow men.

John's new orders sent him to Lake Crystal, where Mr. Alberts found him a nice cabin and where he made his headquarters for almost a year. In that time he went from camp to camp, cooking, supervising, trouble-shooting for the boarding contractor as need arose, but always and eternally preaching Christ and teaching the Word of God.

His fame as a preacher soon equalled his reputation as a cook, and men were as grateful for his sermons as they were glad to get his food. Governor Johnson was elated at the progress and stability of the man on whom he had risked his political future, when he issued that most fateful pardon, and a strong bond of love and mutual appreciation developed between the men. The governor had John fill a pulpit in the Twin Cities whenever the new apostle came that way, and so the fame of the preacher reached beyond his own huge parish.

One other attraction held John at Lake Crystal, a most attractive girl named Matilda Zeills. She was less than half the age of the redeemed outlaw, but she found him a romantic and attractive figure. Dressed in his Sunday-best he was a handsome sight, and in the pulpit he filled the eye as well as the ear. May's father snorted at the idea of a serious affair between the incongruous couple. He was certain that "the child" would get over her silly ideas and that "an old man" like John, who could have been her father, would soon lose his fascination for her. Every time the preacher approached Mr. Zeills to talk to him about his daughter, the father brushed him aside and said, "Nonsense!"

Some wise but unknown person has said that "Life is one fool thing after another: Love is *two* fool things after *each* other." Be that as it may, Mr. Zeills was stunned one morning to wake up and find that Matilda May and John had eloped, and the governor had given the bride away at a hasty ceremony! It was two years before he saw his daughter again, and since the ceremony had been performed by Frank Higgins, with Governor Johnson's blessing, he could only make the best of the situation. So John's wedding was in perfect accord with the general pattern of his whole life. Whatever he did was flavored with adventure and had to be out of the ordinary. May was a grand girl and the perfect wife for John. In addition to helping him in his ministry, she found time to bear him three sons and five daughters, and to give him refuge and sanctuary in a happy home. Often she went to the woods with him, and always he came home to a warm and loving welcome that crowned his hard life with the deep blessing of love and devotion.

He never went back to his cooking job again. Destiny beckoned down a different trail. Once again the wings of adventure fanned his cheeks, but this time it was an adventure of the spirit, for the Kingdom of God.

# The Apostle's Career

# CHAPTER IV

## The Apostle's Career

The newly wedded couple were still honeymooning in Minneapolis when two important communications reached them. One was from Mr. Alberts, who wanted John to cut his vacation short and hurry back to his job, and the other was from the Sky Pilot. His message merely asked John to stay where he was until Frank arrived for a conference, so the honeymoon continued, to the detriment of Mr. Alberts' business. When Higgins reached Minneapolis he was accompanied by a Mr. Coffman from Duluth, who had become interested in John's career.

Frank opened the discussion by saying, "I feel pretty sure that God has a great work for you to do, John, and I want a hand in starting you out properly. I have two hundred dollars to help finance another Sky pilot. Mr. Coffman will put in two hundred more, if you will go to Bigfork for a year, and start a work there. Four hundred a year isn't much to a man who is making $175 a month, but $175 isn't much to a man who has won the prizes you have in the ring. I want you to think this over, and when you make up your mind let me know and I'll give you what help I can.

John asked, "When do I start?"

That was all there was to it, and Frank Higgins had an assistant, an Elisha to Minnesota's Elijah. Thus John became the second of the three great Apostles of the Pines. Three days later he and his wife stepped off the train in

Bigfork, the lewdest, most notorious and lawless town in all the great north country. In the small group which met them at the station was John's dad, who had not yet met his new daughter-in-law. When he met May, Mr. Sornberger shook his head and said, "Girl, you must have wanted to go to a wedding mighty bad!" This fatherly appraisal of John as a bridegroom was the only comment the old man ever made on John's marriage. He never referred to it again.

Bigfork, being the end of the drive, was naturally the mecca for the brawling jacks, who yearned for the fleshpots after a long winter of labor, and who sought for entertainment in all of its most bawdy forms. At that time five out of every seven buildings were devoted to vice in one form or other, and there was no church or religious work of any kind in the entire town. The night was no different from the day, except that it was even noisier. A bawling stream of shouting men surged up and down the streets waving bottles, yelling obscene greeting to all who passed, and making it almost impossible for a sober person to sleep.

Into this pool of iniquity John plunged, head over heels. He rented a vacant store room and opened his campaign to tame Bigfork with the Gospel, having not one chance in a thousand to succeed. The fact that he carried out his plan to a successful conclusion is proof that miracles still occur. When John moved on a few years later, he left behind him a thriving Presbyterian Church, a town that was safe for women and children, and the first and only "dry" town the region had ever known; made so by local option!

When word got around that the notorious Jack McWilliams was preaching nightly in Bigfork he never lacked a crowd, the jacks coming in great numbers to see and hear him. May assisted him in the services, and since the roughest bully in the woods had a regard for women

144

which amounted almost to a superstitious reverence, she walked safely in the wild community. There were some converts every meeting, and the work was quickly on an established basis. Knowing the evils of drink as he had seen them from both sides of the bar, John never missed a chance to strike a blow at the saloon, and before long his ceaseless campaign began to hurt the booze interests. But active animosity did not begin until John invaded the territory of the enemy to rescue a friend from their grasp.

Chancing to be in the railroad station when a train load of jacks came in from the woods, John saw an old-timer he knew and went up to greet him. He was pleased to see John, and after a few minutes conversation said, "Jack, I'd like to ask you to do me a favor."

"Sure," John replied, "anything I can."

"This might get you into trouble," his friend warned.

"In that case," said the preacher, "I sure WILL do it. What is this favor you want?"

Wistfully the man stated his case: "I ain't been home to see my wife and kids for three years. I plan to go every time I come out of the woods. But I get a few drinks in me, then I pass out. When I wake up in a gutter a couple of days later, I'm broke, without a dime in my pants. I can't go home that way, so I go back in the woods and work another six months, and then I do the same thing over again. This time I want it different. Will you see me safe through tonight? Keep me out of the saloons, and get me on that train tomorrow morning."

"You bet I will!" John agreed. "You are as good as home right now, with money in your pockets." He took his friend along home with him, and May had company to feed for supper. Not an unusual situation for the young bride, it may be noted in passing. After the evening meal the three of them went together to the service, where the visitor seemed to enjoy the meeting greatly. But when John was dealing with some converts and talking to some friends at the front, the man slipped out and disappeared. When John missed him he had been gone almost an hour.

Knowing from sad experience what had probably happened, John hurried out to hunt the missing sheep. He went from saloon to saloon, giving each one a hasty search and passing on to the next. In fifteen minutes he located the prodigal, standing at a bar and rapidly getting into a state of alcoholic petrification. John took him by the elbow and said, "That's all, Sam! Drink that one down and we go home."

Sam objected. "I'm a curly wolf," he stated in a voice which shook the rafters, "and it's my night to howl!"

"Howl outside!" John insisted, "I took a contract to load you on a train tomorrow, and I aim to make good," All the while he was propelling the struggling friend toward the door. Attracted by the uproar, the bouncer came hurrying over. "Wot's going on here?" he demanded.

"He wants me to go home," Sam complained, pointing to Jack. "It's my money, and if I want to spend it having a good time, there ain't no . . . preacher going to tell me I can't. Am I right, or ain't I?" he asked the bouncer.

"You BET you're right," the strong-arm gent assured him, "and nobody ain't taking you out o' here while you got a dime to spend!" Then turning to John he ordered, "Outside, you, and STAY out."

John laughed in his face and said, "When I go old Sam goes with me."

Then the bouncer made his big mistake. He swung a mighty roundhouse hook at John, who did not wait for the blow to arrive. He stepped in smoothly and easily and hit the bouncer right on the button. The bruiser did not wake up for ten minutes, which was all the time John needed. He turned to Sam and said, "Are you coming with me?"

His friend had just enough whiskey in him to be stubborn, and he said, "No, I ain't going nowhere!"

"Wrong," said John, "you're going home." Where-

146

upon he calmly hooked Sam on the chin, and Sam joined the bouncer in dreamland. Then the preacher stooped, picked up the limp form of his friend, draped him over his shoulder and started for the door. A bartender picked up a bung-starter and headed around the end of the bar to intercept the muscular good Samaritan, but the owner grabbed his arm and said, "Hold it, you fool! That's Jack McWilliams! He'll kill you. I wouldn't mind that, but I don't want this joint wrecked by a one-man cyclone!"

Sam slept all night in John's house, and when he woke up he was stripped to his underwear. He began calling for his clothes, and John came in laughing and carrying a coffee pot. "Quit bawling!" John said. "You get your pants just twenty minutes before that train leaves!" Sam settled back with a pleased grin and said, "Jack, it looks like I made the grade, and this time I go home!" And when the train pulled out Sam was on it. He was sober, well-heeled with six months pay, and headed for a reunion.

Sam was deeply grateful, but others were not. So a council was called by the ungodly, to consider steps which might be taken to subdue the preacher. The whiskey peddlers were not going to have their business interfered with, without a fight, and since they controlled the local law and politics they were pretty sure they could enforce anything short of murder. The leaders met in the office of one of the saloons and went into conference. The first practical suggestion was typical of the men and their methods: one man proposed to have a gang waylay John in a dark street, club him into unconsciousness, break a few bones, and leave him in a hospital to recover if he could. But a wiser man vetoed the plan on the ground that such action would arouse Governor Johnson, whose friendship for John was well known, and he would supersede the local law and they would be in worse trouble than they had been before they got rid of John.

Finally a plan was hatched that had every prospect of

success. They decided to import a noted young bully from Michigan, whose reputation as a fighter was wide-spread over the northwest. Wherever fighting men gathered they mentioned his name with respect, and he was reputed to be the toughest man outside of the penitentiary. If he would come and give John a first class beating in a fair fight, the preacher would be washed up and his sun set. So, for the modest fee of five hundred dollars, plus the chance to be known as the man who ran Jack McWilliams out of his own home town, the bully was hired.

John, of course, knew nothing of this. The frame-up was almost perfect. The bully arrived quietly and reported for duty. He had John pointed out to him, and began to study his victim. He learned that John and May took a walk every afternoon, looking in the windows of the few shops, and visiting friends. Their route led past the saloon of the ring leader of the plot, the largest center of vice in the town.

Completely at peace with the world, John walked into the trap. On a bright Monday afternoon word went out quietly to a hundred people that this was the day, and they gathered in the chosen arena. The tables were moved out to give the gladiators plenty of room, and the spectators lined up against the wall out of the way. John and May came strolling down the side walk arm in arm, the bully watching from the doorway, concealed by the screen door. When his victim was almost in front of the saloon the bully stepped out casually, placed himself in front of May and said to John, "*Where did you pick up that slut*?" Then he quickly stepped back into the saloon, slipping his brass knuckles on his right hand as the screen door closed behind him.

At the insult to his wife, John went berserk; not noticing that the screen door swung outward, he gave a bellow and plunged after the bully, hitting the door with his shoulder, expecting it to swing open. Instead, it held,

and John went through. He took the light door right off
its hinges and landed in the saloon with the door hung
around his neck. The bully was set to start action, but
couldn't reach John because of his quaint necklace. When
John took hold of the frame and tore it off he swung it
back out of the way with his right hand. He was just exactly
the right distance from the hired fighter, and he finished
the one motion by bringing his right hand around in a
whistling hook. It took the visiting specialist in mayhem
right on the point of the chin, and he sagged to the floor.
Following the rules of that highly specialized game, John
leaped across the man on the floor, booting him in the side
of the head as he crossed over.

Exit one bully.

F*inis:* one fight.

John's leap carried him so close to the bar, however,
one of the bartenders seized what looked like a golden
opportunity. He grabbed a bottle and swung it at the back
of John's head. The alert scrapper saw the motion out of
the corner of his eye, ducked and whirled in one swift
motion. He caught the wrist of his new assailant as the
blow fell, and broke the man's arm on the edge of the bar.
Then he leaped over the bar in one clean vault, hit the
dazed bartender behind the ear, and turned to any new
business which might be before the house.

He grabbed a full bottle of whiskey in each hand and,
with unholy joy, swept the back bar clear of glasses,
bottles, and liquor; thus doing a full thousand dollars
worth of damage to the owner. Then he noticed the men
lined up against the wall—having been too busy to see
them until that moment. He climbed up on the bar, a
broken bottle held like a dagger in each hand, and sent out
his challenge: "All right," he said, "I'll clean up the whole
lousy crew of you." His eye swept up and down the row
as he demanded, "Which end of the line do I begin on?"

One of the audience laughed like a bull and shouted,

"Not me, Jack! I'm only a spectator! I just came to see the fun, and I've sure had MY money's worth! I ain't fighting nobody—especially you."

The decision was unanimous: the fracas was over. The bully was still out cold, and the bartender hadn't yet moved. John casually broke the few bottles which had escaped his first wild sweeps, picked up a heavy beer stein and hurled it through the plate glass mirror, then started for the door. When he reached it he turned. Looking at the crowd, he spat on the floor, and said, "There'll be preaching tonight as usual, and you are all invited." Then he went out to join May, who was still standing where he had left her, wondering if she was a widow.

The old warrior knew a frame-up when he saw one; especially when he was the intended victim. He called his friends together and said, "We have to fight. We can't turn this town over to the forces of Hell and just walk out. We must ask God to lead us and then pitch in and give the devil a licking." Prayer meetings were organized, and John and his small flock started out to gather evidence of violations of the law. In a few days they had plenty of proof that would stand up in court, and John went to see the sheriff. The officer said he would see what could be done, and for four weeks kept out of John's way in spite of all the crusader could do to corner him. But the saloon crowd knew from the sheriff of the campaign against them, and they made one more attempt to intimidate their sworn foe.

A merchant came to John and said, "Preacher, I ain't taking sides in this fracas. I like to be at peace with everybody." John snorted scornfully, but before he could speak the storekeeper continued: "I want to do you a favor. There is some talk about a gang of roughs busting up your meeting some night and smashing all your furniture. You wouldn't like that, now would you?"

"John said, "No, I wouldn't like that, and neither would the fellows that had it done! I also don't like a pussy-footer! Now you go right back to the crooks that sent you on this errand and tell them for me that I've got forty dollars worth of benches in my meeting house, and I'd hate to see them busted up. In fact, I'd feel so bad it that happened, I'd get 500 lumberjacks, arm them with pick handles, and smash every saloon in this town. I'll bet that would cost somebody forty THOUSAND dollars!" The stool pigeon made his report, and no further word was heard from that quarter.

Unable to get any help from the law, John took a trip to St. Paul and had an interview with Governor Johnson. That godly Christian man burned with indignation when John told him of conditions there, and he gave John authority to supersede the sheriff, and armed him with credentials as a special officer representing the governor. He also appointed an honest and fearless man as a special prosecutor, and John and his staunch friends got busy. Some of the wiser saloon keepers saw the handwriting on the wall and sold out while they could. Others moved their stock and equipment to other fields, and in a short time Bigfork was dry. It was transformed into a quiet and peaceful town of homes and orderly business, and a Presbyterian Church took the place of the store room meeting place. It was a proud and happy day for John when he organized that church, the first concrete proof of his great labor for God in that region.

In the meantime he had come under the care of the Presbytery of Duluth as a candidate for the ministry, and in time became ordained as an evangelist. The same ecclesiastical machine which fought Frank Higgins so bitterly lined up to protest John's ordination, and his friends had some difficulty getting it through. The protest was made on the grounds that John was not a graduate of seminary, and could not read Greek or Hebrew. John's reply was simple. He said he would dare any seminary graduate to spend thirty days in the woods with a pack, preaching to the jacks! As for Greek and Hebrew, he said

151

he never met a lumberjack who could understand either language, so he'd just go right on preaching in English! And since certain powerful leaders of the presbytery knew of John's work and were supporting him, there was enough influence behind him to carry him through the crises which animosity continually evoked. Prominent among the staunch friends of John were Mr. Luke Marvin, an elder in the First Presbyterian Church of Duluth; a powerful lumber operator, Mr. George G. Barnum, also a member of the same church, and Mr. Coffman, who had put up half of the funds for the start of the work at Bigfork. Mr. Marvin was quick to do battle for John whenever and wherever it was necessary, and in his notes and records the great lumberjack evangelist made many references to this great Christian statesman, who influenced his own generation so strongly for Christ and His Word. As a ruling elder, Mr. Marvin was often a delegate to the meetings of presbytery, and as an evangelical Christian he was more interested in the salvation of men than he was in strict adherence to denominational rules and procedures. When certain leaders of the presbytery banded together to protest the ordination of an uncouth person, who had never even seen the outside of a seminary, Elder Marvin reminded them how they had opposed Frank Higgins in the same fashion and for the same reason, but after refusing him ordination many times they afterward bragged over the fact that their presbytery did finally accept Frank into the sainted fold! Now they were following the same pattern with John Sornberger, and he was certain God had called this man to a great task, and the presbytery was compelled to heed him in the end.

One of the greatest obstacles to the ordination was John himself! He didn't particularly care whether he became a "Reverend" or not, and he was very impatient under restraint and contemptuous of rules and regulations when they stood in his way. While he was on probation he was asked to make a report to presbytery about the success of his ministry, and in the course of his remarks he casually mentioned the fact that he had baptized over twenty men in one camp. One of John's sponsors, a pastor of an influential church, pulled the speaker's coat tail to stop him. John looked down and asked in a whisper which would have carried across the Mississippi River, "What's the matter? What did I do wrong?"

His friend said, "John, in Presbyterian law and custom a man does not administer the sacraments until he has been ordained. You should not baptize before you are thus qualified."

In the same loud whisper John said, "O.K., Doctor, Presbytery can baptize 'em over again if you think it didn't take—providing you can catch them!" Then he burst out in gargantuan laughter, in which many of the members joined. One of the so-called "liberals" saw a chance to embarrass John's friends, so rose to ask a question.

"Mr. Moderator," he began, "I would like to know if this man has had the effrontery to administer the sacrament of communion also."

John did not hesitate. He said, "I came one night into a pioneer's home where small pox had hit, and they had no doctor and no nurse. I sent a friend down the river in my boat to get a doctor, and I did what I could to help the afflicted ones. In a bed were a woman and a half-grown child, both pretty far gone. In fact, they both died before the doctor arrived. The woman saw my Bible and asked, 'Are you a preacher?' I said I was, and she said, 'I am a Christian and so is my daughter. I feel I could die content if we could take communion once more before I saw the Lord.' Well, sir, I got some crusts of bread and some Dago wine from a jug, and I gave those dying Christians communion. What would YOU have done in the same circumstance?"

There was a hush over the gathering as the men contemplated that picture. The dread scourge from which men then fled in terror reigning in an isolated group of shacks, and one man of God standing by until help came! Not many of them would have had the courage to have remained to offer either spiritual or physical help. One of John's friends saw an opportunity and suggested, "We can avoid future problems like this by the simple process of ordaining this man, on whom the Lord has laid His hand, and who is sealed to his task by the Holy Spirit, Who also called Paul from outside the recognized Christian community. These 'other sheep' need a shepherd. I am convinced John Sornberger is the one. Why do we hesitate to recognize him?" A short time thereafter the dignity was conferred upon the ex-outlaw and he was ordained.

The reformation of Bigfork was a Herculean task, but even so stupendous a job did not absorb all of John's tremendous energy. Even while he battled corruption, fought vice, cleaned up a town and built a church in the wilderness he still found time to carry on work in many of the camps. In the first year he was at Bigfork he covered 381 miles of trail on foot, carrying his pack in fair weather and in foul. In the winter he wore snowshoes and in the summer boots, but he left his imprint on a vast territory. When three years were gone by, Frank felt that John's work at Bigfork could now be entrusted to another man, and he moved John to Ranier, which was then a tough hell-hole near International Falls.

There he stayed for two years, and while he led many men to Christ and did a great work there, he often confessed with chagrin that Ranier licked him—the only situation he was ever in which he could not handle. Nobody could tame that wild cesspool of sin in its palmy days, not even the militia! Al Channer once told me that he had to spend a night in Ranier on one occasion, and secured a room at the hotel. The halls were thronged with streams of rioting drunks, pushing in doors and picking fights all over the hotel. The uproar was so bad Al stated he was afraid to spend a night there, so he took his "turkey" and sat up in the depot until dawn came. Needless to say, John tried his best, but after two years he had to give it up. As fast as he cleaned out one dive two others sprang up. The local politicians controlled the commercialized vice in the city, and were getting rich from the monopoly of evil. Hence the local law officers were no aid, and the sheriff said he would resign before he'd risk his life in that Sodom. The twenty-four months' ministry made no impression on the situation. The individuals who were converted passed on out of town and there was no organized group to back the preacher.

So Frank decided to move John, and gave him a new assignment. He bought him a launch with which to patrol the two great rivers, the Rainy and the Mississippi, preaching to all the camps and mills along the banks of those streams. John had a glorious time, using his launch as a home, a hospital, an ambulance, and often as a pulpit from which he preached to crowds on the bank of the stream. As in all of his ministry, his major theme was regeneration. Rarely did he preach without some visible results. As he carried the Gospel to new sections, he often tied his launch to the bank, took his "turkey" on his back, and hiked forty or fifty miles through the woods to reach out-lying camps. The whole region knew him, and rejoiced when he appeared with his cheerful, fun packed sermons; all of which offered hope for the sinner and help to the weak.

John had moved his wife and family to Duluth, but he stayed in the field which he knew so intimately. Between Virginia and Rainy Lake there were 30,000 men in the woods, and that constituted John's parish. Those men were his congregation. With a territory of thousands of square miles and a congregation of thousands of wild turbulent men, the preacher had more than a hundred pastors could adequately handle. Rest was a stranger to John. His great heart would not let him slow down, and his iron constitution and phenomenal strength carried him through, and grace came to enlighten many darkened minds. A light burned in the camps because of him, and the toughest men in the North were his greatest admirers.

When six years had passed, Higgins came to John and suggested that he leave the woods for brief spells to see what he could do as an evangelist. Frank knew that if revivals could be started in the various cities and towns of the territory the benefits would reach the men in the camps, and he finally persuaded his aggressive associate to try the plan. Since Frank's home was at Delano, the first campaign was held there; all of the local churches cooperating. From the first night it was apparent that a new star had appeared in the firmament of evangelism. John was in his natural environment before a crowd, and the freedom of a revival meeting was exactly what was needed to bring out all his latent powers. Indeed, some of the ministers were afraid this new orb might turn out to be a *shooting* star, and not without reason! He pranced about the platform as though it were a prize ring. He furled defiance at Satan and all of his works and followers. He blasted every form of evil that the community harbored. If his style was unorthodox it was effective, for results were astonishing from the start.

One of the first converts of the Delano meeting was Frank Higgins' own daughter. When the Sky Pilot saw his own beloved child come down the aisle to accept Christ, his cry of joy and praise could be heard for many blocks! From then on John was thrice-beloved by his superior and friend, and the love and labor which Higgins had lavished on John returned like the bread cast upon the waters. Scores of others accepted Christ, backsliders were restored, broken homes were reconciled and enmities of years standing healed and forgotten.

As to his ability in this field, let a newspaper editor be heard. While in the midst of a great campaign, this man wrote in his columns:

"We hear a great deal about Billy Sunday, Wilbur Chapman and Gypsy Smith, but none have more remarkable qualities than Evangelist Sornberger. He possesses to a high degree the characteristics essential to a great evangelist. He is a devoted Christian, a fine organizer, has profound knowledge of human nature and is a great preacher. At one time he is a firebrand, burning the consequences of sin into the soul of men and women; at other times he is as refreshing as an April shower, bringing messages of wonderful tenderness and love, other times he reaches great heights of oratorical power, lifting his listeners to the highest realms of thought and spirit. Back of this preaching is a winning personality, a genial nature, and a likable man. Direct as a business man, impassioned as a lawyer in a great case and as appealing as a father whose children are in peril. At times he is as witty as Sam Jones and as eloquent as Moody, yet different from others in many things, having a combination of rare gifts."

John did not reach this envied position and reputation expressed by the editor without labor and travail. One of his strongest friends in the presbytery was then the pastor at Coleraine, a man of great heart and deep spiritual understanding. John always called his mentor "Daddy" Schwartz, and this scholarly gentleman set out to "make a silk purse out of a sow's ear" as John himself often expressed it. He insisted that John wear a coat in the pulpit, and tried to tame his boisterous gestures and tone down his lurid language. After every sermon the friends would meet and go into a "huddle." John would begin, "Well, Daddy Schwartz, what did I do wrong THIS time?"

The kindly old gentleman would shake his head and say, "Now, John! Now, JOHN!"

The budding evangelist would insist, "Come on, let's have it. What peeved you about the middle of the sermon?

I saw you get a long face and knew I'd done SOMETHING wrong!"

Then the preacher would begin: "The Spirit of God was in that meeting until you climbed up on the railing and offered to lick any man in the crowd who didn't believe in Jesus" or "Until you jumped over the pulpit to show how young and strong you are" or "Until you said, If any man doesn't WANT to go to Heaven, LET him go to Hell!! My son, there is a dignity about the Gospel and the ministry..." And John would get a lecture on deportment and vocabulary which he heeded and through which he profited and advanced. But he never lost his salty language and pithy style of speech. Here are some typical sentences from one of his sermons on "Revivals:"

"Revivals are for Christian people and are not only proper but very necessary. They are according to God's work. 'Wilt thou not revive us again that thy people may rejoice in thee?' cried the psalmist of old and God honored the cry."

"Revival is God's way and it is nature's way, as all plant life revives in the spring, bringing forth bud and blossom and fruit. So God, by His Spirit seeks to kindle into flame the smoking flax. The church that has no revival dies of spiritual dry rot."

"Some Christians think they are good enough without a revival. Well, some are so good they are good for nothing. Some are so slow in God's service they can't stop quick!"

"Some preachers seen to be fitted to preach funeral sermons only. If one were not standing and the other lying down, it would be hard to tell which was the corpse."

"The devil is traveling so fast he exceeds the speed limit while the speed of some preachers enables them to see only his tail lights."

"God says 'present your bodies a living sacrifice,' not a dead one. He says, 'Rejoice in the Lord,' not moan and groan."

"I am afraid of that long-faced, sanctified, holier-than-thou look. I fear that look is trying to cover up some deviltry. That person needs a revival."

"But some are opposed to revivals. So is the devil."

"Some say revivals are sensational, they cause too much excitement. When I can't shout as long and loud and be as enthusiastic for the King of Kings as I would be at a ball game, I'll quit preaching."

After the sensational revival at Delano, John went back into the woods again, for although he was destined to travel widely and address great throngs all over the country, he never forgot his first love, and always longed to be back in the camps with his "boys." So while Frank was setting up another evangelistic meeting, John's launch was plying the rivers and his feet were treading wild trails. He gathered a fine group of converts at Jacobson, and in the course of time a thriving Presbyterian church was established there, although John himself was not the founder. Later, when the mines opened at Keewatin he also organized and built a church there, and all of his churches are functioning still.

Six years of sober, godly living, combined with the rigors of his outdoor life had changed the man outwardly even as the Spirit of God had renewed him inwardly. His eyes were keen and clear, the marks of sin and dissipation had disappeared from his countenance, and the only permanent effect of his wild years was a slight limp—due to his broken leg, and the stray bits of lead in his system. He carried five bullets in his body to his grave. On the platform he made a handsome picture of virile manhood, and the photographs of the young evangelist show a magnetic personality. He maintained a vigorous schedule. I have before me as I write clippings from old newspapers which contain accounts of some of his early campaigns. "The Aitkin Republican" tells of the closing day of his sweeping revival in that city, and lists his services for the last day as follows:

9:00 a.m. Sermon to the Baptist Sunday School.
11:00 a.m. Sermon to Calvary Baptist Church.
2:45 p.m. Mass meeting for men.
7:30 p.m. Sermon at Congregational Church.
8:30 p.m. Closing Sermon at Calvary Baptist Church.

This same newspaper asserts that his campaign had resulted in the greatest spiritual awakening the city of Aitkin had ever seen, and was filled with praise of his preaching.

Other communities were equally enthusiastic, as John made it a point of honour to conduct campaigns in every northwestern state where the law had hunted him, and where warrants had been issued for his arrest. His revivals laid hold on the imagination of the public of that day, and listeners followed his sermons with delight. This pleasure was due partly to the charm of the man, but more particularly to the bold and clear Gospel he proclaimed. A typical editorial evaluation of the man and his message may be seen in a clipping from a Sherburn paper, during a revival to which people traveled from three states. I reproduce it here in a facsimile, giving only the opening paragraph:

"This is the last week of the special evangelistic meetings at the Sherburn Gospel Tabernacle. The success of the meeting so far has exceeded all anticipations. Last Sunday Evangelist Sornberger preached at three services, the tabernacle being filled at every meeting. The evening service was outstanding in its evangelistic appeal. Following a mighty message by the evangelist touching on the necessity of the "being born again" experience, the church was privileged to witness an old time Wesleyan altar response. The evangelist brought out scriptural truths most convincingly and emphatically. The great thing about John Sornberger's preaching is the fact that he doesn't beat about the bush. He doesn't sugarcoat his sermons to please society butterflies, poker sharks, bootleggers or milk maids. He preaches the un-adulterated gospel of repentance and salvation, and he is not playing any favourites. The higher up they are in the pink tea circles of society the better the old gospel fits them, he maintains."

Editors were fond of John. He was "good copy" and they liked his blunt honesty. Impressed with the repetition of his life theme in the great revival which swept their community, the editor of the "Cavalier Chronicle" dubbed the evangelist "Twice-born John," and the name stuck. The preacher accepted this as a compliment, since it epitomized his entire message and carried the suggestion of the Gospel he preached. So his fame spread. Crowds thronged to hear him, and throughout all of the acclaim and attention he never changed. He was the lumberjack preacher to the end.

Between his city campaigns he returned again and again to the woods. His family was growing and often he took the whole brood with him on tour. The children loved these trips, as the woods were their favorite playground. On the trail, his wife and two older children walked with him, and the baby rode in a pack on his father's back. John just cut two holes in the corners of a knapsack for the tiny legs to stick out, and the child rode like a papoose, viewing the world in reverse as he rode backward.

On one trip the blacksmith in one of the camps heard the sky pilot preach, and after the service called him into the shop. There he confessed that drink had so degraded him that he had deserted his wife and family twelve years before, and had never felt fit to go back to them. John led the man to Christ, and the new convert, born again, laid aside his sin and weakness for booze, returned to his family and started life anew. He lived for years a respected citizen of Minnesota, and died greatly mourned by the family with whom Christ had reconciled him. This, incidentally, was not a unique occasion in John's ministry. He had a list of thirty-two such homes which were salvaged by the Gospel he preached. Seven of his converts entered the ministry in the first six years of his preaching career, and he left his mark on at lest two generations of woodsmen.

In all of this, Adventure had not forgotten him. He remained her darling to the end. His life in the woods was hazardous enough, but still he went out of his way, apparently, to hunt new risks. One of the episodes which made his name a legend in the North is reported rather fully in the columns of "The Daily Times-Herald" of Fort William, Ontario, for the date of September 14, 1921. At the time John's family was living on the small farm which Higgins had bought for John at Munger, Minnesota. John heard of a tragedy which had occurred to a friend, Mr. Robert R. Harris, of Spokane, Washington. Vacationing in Isle Royal, in Lake Superior, Mr. Harris had set out from Rock Island Lodge in an open boat, on a fishing expedition. A fierce gale blew up suddenly, and the fisherman was never seen again. While the excitement of the search was at its height, John heard of his friend's disappearance, so he took passage on the Steamer Noronic to Fort William, a point of departure for the island.

When he arrived he identified himself to the port officials, and they welcomed his help because of his reputation as a woodsman and guide. John got the weather reports for the date of the gale, studied the direction and velocity of the wind and computed the probable drift of a small boat under the conditions which prevailed. He asserted that it had to be in one of four places: Thunder

Cape, Silver Islet, Swede Island, or Point Magnet. The authorities put the tug "Gracie" at his disposal, under the command of Captain Seagel, and guided by John they set out.

Like a homing pigeon John led the small expedition to the exact spot where the small boat was beached and wrecked by the waves. They never recovered the body of the lost man, but the story was all too clear, for pencilled on the side of the boat was the man's last message. Chilled, battered, and weakened as he clung desperately to the gunwale of the submerged boat, Mr. Harris had taken a pencil from his pocket and scrawled his words of farewell. He told of his plight and weakened helplessness, bade his wife and son Bobbie farewell, and was swept away by the fierce seas. The writing was upside down, due to the man's position in the water, but legible and clear.

Fire, also, played its part in his adventurous career. The people of Minnesota will long remember the terrible forest fire which began on October 12, 1918, and swept a vast area with death and devastation. Hundreds of persons perished, thousands of square miles of timber, farm land, and cultivated crops were swept by fire, and millions of dollars worth of damage resulted. John and his family were then well established in their homestead at Munger, he being one of the first to pioneer that region. He lost his home and everything he possessed in this world in the awful holocaust, and he and his family escaped as though by a miracle.

The summer had been disastrously dry. No rain had fallen for months. The drought was general all over the region, and the very air was super-heated and seemed almost ready to ignite. Whether the tragedy was really caused by a spark from a locomotive, a careless smoker, the sun shining through a glass bottle in the dry grass, or a flicker of summer lightning no one can say with certainty. But one of the most awful fires ever seen suddenly began to roar down toward the lake. It swept over Munger, Cloquet, Moose Lake, and a score of other settlements and reached the suburbs of Duluth.

Driven by a wind which reached a velocity of sixty-five miles an hour, the blaze split and became two fires. One huge tongue of flame raced over Scanlon, Cloquet, Woodland, and reached the Boulevard in Duluth where it was halted by heroic work. The other sea of fire wiped out Kettle River and Moose Lake, and followed the general direction of the right-of-way of the Moose Lake and Kettle River Railroad, being halted only by the north shore of the lake.

There was nothing like it in the history of the north woods. The air was opaque with ashes, super-hot and electric. It was the type of conflagration all woodsmen dread, a "crown blaze." It did not creep along the ground, feeding on brush and slowed down by green growth, but it leaped from tree-top to tree-top, often hurling itself across a half mile of space in one huge jump. Great balls of gas formed in the air and rolled ahead, exploding with devastating results. They looked like lightning when they detonated and sounded like giant cannon, and they caused the fire to travel faster than a speeding automobile could keep ahead of it! Buildings a half mile from any timber suddenly exploded into flames, and there was no place of refuge. The wind increased to the strength of a tornado, and men fled from danger into the jaws of death, with no way of escape. Two days after the fire, rain fell in torrents, followed by snow and extreme cold, and the suffering was indescribable.

When the fire drew near Munger, John and his family took refuge in the railroad station, waiting for a train to carry the fleeing settlers to safety. But the depot caught fire before the train arrived, and they fled in autos as best they could. John was separated from his wife and children, and worked like a giant to help other men's wives and babes. But for two weary days and nights he never knew whether his own loved ones had perished or not, and when they were reunited in Duluth almost by accident he could only clasp them to his heart and thank God that they had all escaped. All of their possessions were gone: home, barns, stock, implements, furniture and clothes. They owned just what they were wearing when they fled. However, they were all alive and nothing else mattered to the intrepid and heroic family.

John found plenty to do in the days that followed. He was so well known he decided to capitalize on his personal popularity, and became a one-man committee of relief. From all the places where he had conducted revivals he begged clothing, furniture, equipment, and anything the refugees could use. He literally collected TONS of garments, and started a custom which he never thereafter departed from—the distribution of used clothing to the needy. Until death claimed him he had a huge number of women's circles gathering garments for him, and they provided everything from layettes for new babies to wool socks for granddads!

One day John had a call from Governor Johnson, asking him to come to St. Paul to meet a man named Bryan. The renowned Commoner was planning to gather a group of twelve notable temperance lecturers to tour America and advocate the adoption of prohibition, and the governor persuaded the astute Bryan that John belonged on that team. So Bryan agreed to interview the ex-outlaw and look him over.

They met at a lunch arranged by the governor, who was always proud to display John as a trophy of grace. Bryan was attracted to John at once, as the shrewd politician abhorred sham and pretence, and John was real and unassuming. During the lunch the governor said, "John, what is this story you are telling around? It has to do with dynamite, and a man told me you just called the tale 'He moved!' "

"Governor," said John, "he sure did!" He stopped to laugh heartily and then began his account:

"Seven years ago a big husky lumberjack, named Joe Daniels, a hard-drinking fellow, was converted at one of my meetings. Needless to state, after his conversion he was as much opposed to booze as he was in favor of it before conversion. Later he married a pioneer's daughter, bought a forty-acre tract of cut-over land and built a home. Two children (both boys) were born to brighten their home. When these boys were about four and six years of age (that was last summer) a neighbour, who was a good friend of this family but at times a hard-drinking fellow, came to Joe's place one day very drunk. Joe tried to get him to leave, but he insisted on staying and lay down on a home-made settee just outside the house under some pine trees. Joe, hoping to get him into the woods to sleep off his jag, coaxed him to take a walk with him. Although Joe lives far back in the woods off the road, he feared someone might come along and Joe did not like the idea of anyone seeing this drunken fellow around his place. But coax as he might, the fellow refused to stir, so Joe went to a little log store-room where he kept his dynamite. He emptied all the dynamite out of the stick and replaced it with dirt, placed a piece of fuse in the casing and pressed the stiff paper wrapper in place. He went over to the settee and said, "Well, old timer, if you'll not move I'll move you." Joe's two little boys were standing near. Joe lit the fuse, placed it under the settee. Turning, Joe started on the run, at the same time yelling to his boys to run for their lives. As the fellow heard Joe yell to the boys and saw Joe and his boys running for the woods, he looked down and saw what was evidently a stick of dynamite with lighted fuse hissing and smoke issuing from it. He let out a yell that would have made a Comanche Indian green with envy. He jumped to his feet and when he struck the ground he struck it running. He needed no urging to take to the woods. He yelled once or twice as he ran across the clearings. As he crashed through the brush, he took one wild-eyed look backward and disappeared. His wife is still wondering how it was that within an hour after he left home very drunk he returned very much excited and perfectly sober."

Mr. Bryan shouted with laughter, and wiped tears from his eyes. He said, "I'll BET he moved! John, that's one of the funniest stories I ever heard! Do you mind if I use it?"

"Not at all," replied generous John. "Everybody steals my stories. It's quite a change to have an HONEST man ask for one of them!"

The politician chuckled with delight and said, "You'll do, and if Higgins will give you a leave of absence, and ex-governor Hanly consents, I want you on my Flying Squadron."

So John turned from the woods again for a long number of weeks, and the great cities of America heard him with delight. He had no second-hand ideas about liquor: he had served it as a bartender and consumed it as a customer. Whiskey had robbed him of fame and fortune, and made of him a hunted beast. He told his story with graphic effect, and his oratory, combined with the factual data, made him a power in every rally and campaign. So his reputation grew and his fame spread, and he stayed with the distinguished company until they disbanded; their task done. During that time he made powerful friends, who stuck to him until he was buried or until they preceded him Home.

With enhanced prestige and a wider knowledge of national affairs and world leaders, the sky pilot returned gladly to his beloved woods and woodsmen. When he left the north country for wider and more crowded fields, he was always restless and distressed of spirit and yearned to get back where he felt he belonged. Just as Paul knew himself to be called to make God's grace known to the despised Gentiles, so John knew he was elected to be an apostle to the men of the woods. For generations they had been forgotten by the church, and until Frank Higgins began his epochal labors there was very little spiritual help offered them. They were condemned for their way of life, but not shown any better way! Their sins were on a par with their world. They fought timber, snow, blizzard, high water, and huge spaces. They played and sinned on the same cosmic scale. So they scared orderly people out of their orbit, and only one who knew them and was related to their style of existence could touch them with the Gospel.

There is, of course, only one effective message to sinners in any time, place, or degree of need. "Christ died for our sins according to the Scripture," was the way Paul proclaimed it, and nothing else has ever worked from that day to this. But while the MESSAGE never changed, the METHOD of proclaiming it must vary with different circumstances and people. John's method of preaching was simple and forceful. He depended upon logic and ordered reasoning to carry his point. He enlivened his discourses with native wit and a rare humor, and clinched his message with the unanswerable demonstration of his own personal experience. To a young man trained in a seminary the Gospel may be theoretical and debatable: to an outlaw, reclaimed by Christ, it was an effective and trustworthy face, proved by a living and walking miracle.

Out of a hundred or more outlines of John's "barrel" which I have in my present possession, let me offer a typical sample. As you look it through, you must remember that this is just a bare outline from which "the piney apostle" preached. But you can see the logic, the development of an idea based on reason, and the homely illustrations taken from nature and the field of daily life. They are all based upon common experiences with which a lumberjack would be familiar. The theme was John's favorite subject:

## "The New Birth"

Text: John 3:7.
"Ye MUST be born again."
The Bible definite and final.
Leaves no loopholes to crawl out.
Offers no grounds for doubt.

★ ★ ★ ★ ★

The words of the text are from the lips of the
    world's greatest authority.
Jesus: said what He meant;
    meant what He said!

★ ★ ★ ★ ★

He put all the emphasis on "YE MUST!"

★ ★ ★ ★ ★

Nicodemus sought the interview. Note the man:
    was no ignoramus
    was an educated ruler, a lawyer

★ ★ ★ ★ ★

Jesus did not feel flattered, take the visit as a
    compliment, or say, "It is an honour to meet
    you, Governor."
He came right to the point and said, "Ye must be
    born again!"

★ ★ ★ ★ ★

Jesus says the same to every living soul today.
He offers no other way into Heaven
The natural man tries to evade this.
Some say it is not reasonable to make salvation
    depend on something they can't understand
    —can't explain.

★ ★ ★ ★ ★

Tell them nobody understands MUCH of anything!

When animals eat grass, it turns into pork, mutton or beef—why?

On one animal it becomes hair, on the second bristles, on the third wool. Can you explain this?

★ ★ ★ ★ ★

A robin lays a BLUE egg—the robin is brown and red.

A yellow canary lays a WHITE egg.

Can you explain that?

★ ★ ★ ★ ★

The radio and telephone work by electricity: who knows what electricity is?

Electric lights depend on a power plant. Now, even if the lights and the plant are o.k., if you cut the wire there is no light!

Jesus is the cord between God, the power plant, and the Christian, who is the light. You can't let your light shine unless Jesus connects you to God: to get connected you have to be born again!

★ ★ ★ ★ ★

ALL birth is a mystery!

What is born of flesh HAS TO BE flesh:

Spirit produces spirit!

The contrast is as great as darkest night and brightest day.

★ ★ ★ ★ ★

Nothing else works!

Some try to solve spiritual problems by principles of science: but science, limited to FINITE problems, cannot solve INFINITE mysteries.

★ ★ ★ ★ ★

Honesty: virtue: education: the Golden Rule:
These are not the New Birth and cannot take its
   place. All these are fine, but they will not pry
   open the gate to the Kingdom of God.

★ ★ ★ ★ ★

This can be easily illustrated in many ways:
1—My pump quits working, although there is
   plenty of water in the well.
      I pull the pump, clean out the rust, paint it nice
   and shiny, and it still won't work!
      Same old pump.
      *But I put in a new valve,* and now it is o.k. The
   new birth is that new valve! It creates in us a new
   heart and a workable spirit.

★ ★ ★ ★ ★

2—I have a bitter plum tree on my farm–fruit no
   good. What shall I do?
   a) PRUNE IT. Well, that's education: the plums
      are no better.
   b) SPRAY IT. That's culture, good works: but
      bum fruit.
   c) FERTILIZE IT. That's kindness, charity. Still
      bitter plums.

★ ★ ★ ★ ★

   d) God says: "Cut it down and graft on a sweet
      plum!" When I do THAT the bitter tree bears
      sweet fruit!

★ ★ ★ ★ ★

You can't get "better plums" off Adam's seed!
The natural man is carnal.

God's Spirit, which comes when we are born again,
makes all the difference.
NOTHING but this ingrafting of the Holy Spirit
gives us new birth. It changes our nature.

★ ★ ★ ★ ★

God is no respecter of persons: Millionaire or hobo,
unwise or learned, ignorant or educated, refined
or rough-neck—ALL must be born again.

★ ★ ★ ★ ★

A smart man will take God at His Word. He says,
"Now is the acceptable time" and "My Spirit
will not always strive with men."

★ ★ ★ ★ ★

"There is a time, we know not when,
A place, we know not where,
That seals the destiny of men
For glory or despair.
There is a line by us unseen
That crosses every path,
It is the boundary line between
God's mercy and God's wrath."

★ ★ ★ ★ ★

An outline is necessarily a cold and formal thing: the dead skeleton of what may be a warm and living message. So the reader cannot sense the power of John's delivery in the words of the printed form. The sturdy apostle hailed each preaching opportunity as "a slugging match with Satan" as he himself expressed it, and he pulled no punches. To understand how his sermons affected the jacks you would have to see him in action. His eyes would flash with determination or twinkle with humor, he would drive home each point with a fist that made the pulpit shake, and he would denounce sin in scathing terms and

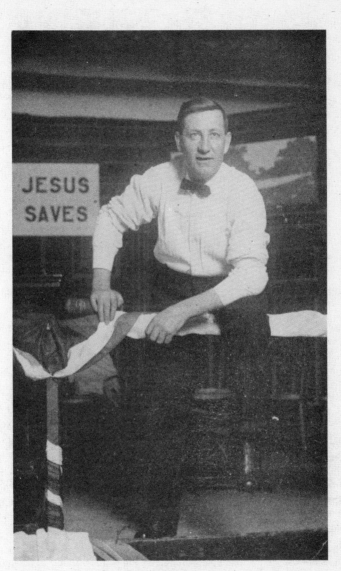

John Sornberger
The Evangelist in Action

John Sornberger Snow Shoeing        John Sornberger Arrives

Hauling Pulpwood to the Landing

plead tenderly with sinners. His style was natural, unspoiled and effective, and no one heard him without being deeply moved. His friends adored him and his enemies hated him, but all agreed on his platform ability.

The dark shadow of Higgins' death covered all of the north woods, but no one felt the sorrow like John Sornberger. To him it was more than the death of a great leader. He had lost one who was at once his spiritual father, his brother, his leader, and his companion in labor. He was all but stunned by the event, and only his faith in God and his great love for the jacks kept him going. He knew that the boys in the camps would be deeply affected by the death of their sky pilot, so he packed his "turkey" and hit the trails, assuring the men by his presence that the work of the Gospel would go on.

But with the death of Frank Higgins the mantle which had been his was now available for some other to wear. Since the work was of God it could not fail, and the Spirit of God alone could pick the proper successor. Realizing the value of the work Higgins had originated and successfully operated, the General Assembly appointed a man from Pennsylvania to succeed Frank in the supervision of the work in the field. The sole qualification of the new appointee was the fact that he had known Higgins. He was an utter stranger to lumberjacks, lumber camps, river drives and all the boisterous background of the wild breed he was supposed to evangelize and tame with the Gospel. This newcomer was appointed to serve for one year, but even though equipped to function as a pastor in a tame and civilized East, he found the wilds of the great north woods another and more difficult problem. However, he met John, and realizing the colour and picturesque appeal of the camp apostle, he took the ex-outlaw to General Assembly and introduced him to the church at large.

John was an instant and huge success, and the Board

of National Missions seized upon him and sent him on a tour, raising money for the Board. John's fiery personality, his wit and sincerity appealed to the throngs who heard him, and for a while he continued in this deputation work. Then, rightly or wrongly, he became convinced that the secretaries of the Board were exploiting him for their own purposes, and he kicked over the traces. He offered to fight any of them, and when there were no takers he challenged the whole crowd! Disgusted and disgruntled he returned to his woods, and went back to his task of preaching in the camps. He refused to work under the man who was the nominal head of the work which Higgins had begun, and since he was too hot for the Board to handle, they dropped the package in the lap of the Presbytery of Duluth. Presbytery acted with wisdom and dispatch in promptly appointing John Sornberger the head and director of the lumberjack work in Minnesota, the birthplace of the work, and the mantle of "Elijah" Higgins came to rest on "Elisha" Sornberger; just where it belonged.

With the mantle came also a seven-fold portion of the Spirit, and great days were in store for the woods apostle. He was free to choose his own field and erect his own program, and all of the true men of the presbytery were proud to help him whenever he called on them for aid. He went on his way blithely, never missing an opportunity and preaching Christ with such vigor and winsome power that a fire burned in his entire huge parish. Since he had the standing given by the appointment of presbytery, he organized a drive among all of the presbyterials in the Synod of Minnesota, and had the godly women collecting tons of used clothing for him. This he distributed among the pioneers and homesteaders freely, and relieved may cases of want and distress. His canoe gave place to another launch, and as the country changed and roads were built he acquired a second-hand car, which was transportation, habitation, ambulance and relief truck all rolled into one.

Nothing tickled John more than to load an expectant mother into the back of his car and start for a distant hospital. He clamped his huge thumb on the horn button, set his foot on the gas, and never lifted either until he stopped in front of the doctor's door or the hospital entrance. He took all curves in high and let all traffic get out of his way, and then would beam and chuckle as he related his "race with the stork" and tell how he beat the bird by several hundred yards! There is no record of how his passengers felt, but having ridden through the woods with John on many occasions, I can imagine their feelings. He used to chuckle and say, "There are all sorts of ways of starting a revival, and many a feller who hasn't thought of God for years has started praying when he took a ride with me."

So a short period of peace settled over the career of the "Stormy Petrel of the Gospel," and his work prospered. Souls were saved and communities blessed until 1920, when another storm-cloud gathered. A member of presbytery came to Elwyn Channer and said, "Al, I know that you are a close friend of John Sornberger, and I just learned something he ought to know. The modernists in the presbytery have framed up a scheme to fire him from his job and put some other fellow in. Failing in that, they plan to close the work entirely. You had better warn him what to expect."

Al consulted with John, and together they went to see the pastor, and some of the session of the First Presbyterian Church in Duluth. These men were tired of being constantly on the alert to protect John and his great ministry, so they said, "There is just one way to settle this. Let us take John on our staff as our woods missionary. We will pay his salary and take care of him, and he will not be under any authority except his own and the Holy Spirit." So John went on the pay-roll of that great church, and they supported him entirely until he died. In the years that he worked under this happy and amicable arrangement he stormed the strongholds of Satan, and set free the captives of his will. He brought light in dark places, and turned the feel of wild men from the path of Hell into the Heavenly way. He continued to be the apostle to the lumberjacks, and even though the years began to slow him down to where he could only do the work of three men instead of five, he never faltered nor rested. I often went to the woods with him, and we preached to the men in the camps. Between meetings we fished and hunted; and John was ready to fight with fists, feet, or axe handles if I tried to do so much as chop wood for the fire! He cooked the meals (and SUCH meals they were! He never lost his culinary skill), made the camp, washed the dishes and insisted that I rest a while! Then when the time came for the services, we stood together while he got his motley crew quiet for the message. To the glorious end of his career he was desperately determined to bring the good news of the new birth to the shaggy thousands who worked and lived far from the church and its influence, to that end he was called and ordained.

In a very real sense, John Sornberger never died, any more than did the Apostle Paul, who lives today in his fourteen epistles, and in the lives of the millions who find Christ through the New Testament. We DO have "Apostolic Succession" in Protestant evangelism, and "The Apostle John of the North Woods" left a valiant and numerous company to continue his great testimony. To this extent he cannot die.

Nor did this hero of the Cross ever quit. He just got so tired that on the 3rd of May, 1939 (69 years of age) he went Home for a rest. There he awaits the hour of the rapture and the return of the Lord, remembered and revered by many. His entrance into Heaven must have been a great occasion, and the happiness that was his when he saw the Christ he served so long and so well beggars description. His funeral sermon on II Timothy 1:12, was preached by Al Channer, as was so eminently fitting, and the church which he fathered at Bigfork commemorated his passing in a great memorial service.

So the mantle was available for some other prophet, and fluttered about for a landing place, but not for long. God had His man ready and prepared, and almost before it had a chance to cool, "the mantle" settled on the one man in this world who had the best right to wear it. Of him we'll now read.

# BOOK THREE

## The Last of the Giants

BOOK THREE

The Last of the Giants

# The Inheritor of the Mantle

# CHAPTER I

# The Inheritor of the Mantle

The little town of Kelsey, Minnesota has always been a lively settlement. Surrounded in the early days by great stands of timber, it was a natural center for lumberjacks and their interests. With rich farm lands nearby, it became a mecca for pioneers who desire to homestead and raise their families on free land, and the commerce that flowed by road and river passed through this thriving place. The men and women who made up the population of the region were hardy folks from whom the best citizens and builders of the state derived their descent and their sterling qualities, and the boys and girls were no strangers to hard work. In the rough days of the turn of the century youth played with the same fervor that marked the labours of the day, and the boys were men almost before they graduated to long pants. A fight or a frolic were one and the same to them, and life was uncomplicated and real.

Seven youths combined their resources, their skill, and their muscles and built at their own expense a crude but adequate dance hall, in which the young folks could have their Saturday night and holiday frolics. Dancing was of the barn dance variety, and consisted more of athletic exercise than grace, but it could generally be said that each dance ended with justification of the phrase, "A good time was had by all." There may have been a few fights during the evening, but that was part of the program and contributed to the joy of the occasion. Generally speaking, the principals in the sudden battles enjoyed them as much as did the spectators!

Two of the "dance hall" proprietors were lads known as "Al" and "Herb." They were the leaders in most of the fun and devilment which highlighted the social activities of the time and place. The town had one general store, which stocked everything from toothpicks to railroad ties, and sold shoes and pins, rifles and coffee, calico and ammunition, and in fact was ready to pass across the counter anything a customer called for, including a coffin! There was also a small railroad depot, which was about fifteen feet square, a section house where the crew slept and boarded, and the famous dance hall built by the boys. This made up the "town"!

A tavern keeper tried to build and operate a saloon there, but he was careless enough to build it on ground owned by the logging company. The proprietor stocked his bar and advertised a grand opening, with free drinks for all comers up to noon on the opening day. He did a rushing business until eleven fifty-nine, when the sheriff walked in, closed the saloon, and put a padlock on the door. That ended the tavern, and none has ever functioned there since! The reason can be traced to a revival that was held there a while after this, and the people have never tolerated any liquor in the town since. Later, a church was formed, and a building erected. It was so small it would not seat over sixty-five people; yet out of that tiny congregation seven men went into the ministry! This constituted the "Town" of Kelsey in 1901, when Mr. William Channer, a professional butter maker, his wife, and ten children came to swell the population.

The business of the small center came from lumberjacks, the railroad crews, and the score of families who had homesteaded around the vicinity, including the Channer family. There were five boys and five girls who

184

bore the name of Channer; the second eldest brother being the one who was christened "Elwyn" but was always known as "Al". Mr. Channer's health had failed and he left the creamery for the north woods, where Al and his elder brother Marvin took over the support of the tribe. At this time Al was just fifteen, which enabled him to count himself a man, do a man's work, and get a man's pay.

The senior Channer took a contract to log out a tract of timber, and the boys did the work. Al was a genius with horses, so the teaming fell largely to him. Mrs. Channer cooked for the camp, and every one of the ten children soon learned to take a turn at the range, and became capable camp cooks. Al was almost six feet tall at the age of fifteen, and weighed 176 pounds. When he filled out at the age of twenty, he topped the scales at 236 pounds, but as a lad his long arms hung down almost to his knees, and were finished off with huge hands that could span nine inches without stretching. He had to wear mittens in the cold weather because gloves were not made in his size, but when those huge hands grasped the reins of a four-horse team, the horses knew who was boss, and gave the driver all they had to give! Those long arms were corded with muscle, and when his cant-hook gripped a log and he threw his weight and strength into the task of rolling that log, either the log or the handle had to give in a hurry!

When Al expressed his ambition to own a farm and conduct a dairy, his dad took up a quarter section of land under the homestead law; eighty acres for himself and eighty for his son. There was a river between the land and the road, and no bridge spanned the stream, so whenever they came or went that river had to be forded. To get a stake to start his dairy, young Al went to work for other logging contractors, using his father's team. The going rate of pay would seem small to us: a teamster received a dollar a day and his board, and got another dollar for a two-horse team, which the company also fed. In view of the fact that a common labourer or swamper received sixteen dollars a month, a dollar a day was relatively high pay for the times.

But a sickly father and eight younger brothers and sisters can make inroads even into an income as regal as a dollar a day, and until the day he married the boy never cashed one pay check for himself. It all went into the family exchequer.

When Al had been thus working in the woods for four years, a tremendous event occurred which drove cows and dairies out of Al's mind. The Dass family moved to Kelsey to take up a homestead. There would have been nothing startling about this had it not been for Bessie, a buxom lassie of sixteen. Al took one look and never recovered! He courted her for five years, ably opposed by his chum, Herb, and they married when Bessie was 21. Al was 24. But much water was to run under the bridge of life before this came to pass, and fathers and mothers kept a sharp eye on their daughters when Al, Herb, and the rest of the group were in town for their weekly frolics.

So passed the years until Al was twenty-one, which year proved to be the pivot of his life. He was working eight miles out of Kelsey, with his team contracted to a jobber who had sub-contracted to clean out a tract of timber. As they worked fourteen hours a day, and more if the light made it possible to see, Al got home once a week only, on Saturday night. Then by Monday morning he was back in time to begin his labours with the first streak of breaking day. This camp was run by a Portuguese named Pedro, ably assisted and abetted by his wife, Maria. It was one of the toughest camps in Minnesota, and one of the most immoral. Since Pedro worked on a contract, all the money he got over and above the expense of the project constituted his profit, and he used every means of increasing his income. His wife, Maria, was the cook and the power behind Pedro. Any shrewd trick he did not think up she was able to concoct, and morals meant absolutely nothing to them. As the men ate their meals, Pedro circulated around the dining room telling them filthy stories at which they laughed with delight, and Maria occasionally poked her head in out of the kitchen to tell one even worse. Pedro kept a jug handy and did a private business as a bootlegger, one which brought back to him as clear profit a fair percentage of the wages he paid some of the men.

One of his common tricks saved him a great deal of money, with the connivance of his wife. She was a striking beauty, with coal black hair, flashing dark eyes, and a figure which she paraded shamelessly before the men to their great delight. When Pedro had occasion to hire a hand for a short time, whom he had to pay at a higher rate, the cunning couple would work a new variation of the old "Badger Game" on their victim. When the special job neared completion, Maria would begin to shine up to the employee, and involve him in a serious flirtation. When she had the "sucker" in the proper mood, Pedro would announce that he would be out of camp that night, and Maria would seek out the victim of her wiles and invite him to share her cabin during her husband's absence. The poor dupe would appear at what he thought was an assignation meeting, and the couple would start to undress. Then Pedro would descend upon them with a shot-gun, roaring with simulated rage, and trying to kick down the front door. The frightened jack would dash out the back door and take off across the country like a deer, and of course never returned for his pay.

Then Maria and Pedro would sit down and roar with laughter, counting up the extra profit they thus made while they congratulated each other over a drink. The lumberjacks who watched this gag worked again and again always kept still when they saw another victim being ripened for the kill, since it appealed to their perverted sense of humour to see the drama enacted. Now bear all this in mind, remembering the character of this couple, as it is important later in the record.

Al came into Kelsey on one certain Saturday night to learn that a revival meeting was being held in the dance hall of which he was a part owner, so no dance could be held. A missionary of the American Sunday School Union conducted the services with the aid of a Presbyterian evangelist, and the whole surrounding region was being stirred. There being nothing else to do, Al and his friends went to the service, and were extremely impressed. He said to himself, "That fever is catching. If a man watched enough of his friends go forward for salvation, he would want to do it himself! But that bird can't catch me, I'll be safe in the woods tomorrow!"

As the service closed the preacher announced that, owing to the illness of his wife, he would have to close the services on Thursday night and leave for home. Al grinned with relief, knowing that he would be in the deep woods until the following Saturday night. As the young folks left the service they agreed that salvation was a good thing, that some of the older ones probably needed it, but their interest was purely academic. Sunday morning he was on his way back to the woods and his work, thinking he had seen the last of the preacher and had heard the last of the revival. He chuckled at the idea of the community dance hall having been used as a revival center, but heartily approved of the action of his partners in lending it rent free for religious purposes. It was certainly a far different use than the hall had been planned for, and the idea appealed to his sense of humor.

Monday and Tuesday and Wednesday went by as usual, just fourteen hours of man-killing labor, three meals that would sink the average office worker so deep he would never float again, eight hours of the sodden sleep which comes to the exhausted, then up to another round of labour. But Wednesday night saw a departure from the routine, by virtue of one of the frequent accidents which somehow seem to lurk around logging camps just waiting to happen to somebody!

One of the common tools of the woods is the huge saw used in felling trees and in cutting them into the proper length for hauling to the mill. This tool may be anywhere from seven and a half to twelve or fourteen feet long, and the huge teeth are kept as sharp as razors. In each camp one skilled man is employed as saw-filer, and it is his task to keep the saws sharpened and set. As a general safety rule these saws, when not in use, are kept in the saw-filer's shack, but on this occasion someone had violated the rule. A careless jack had leaned a newly sharpened saw up against the side of the cook shack and had gone in to eat his supper. In the darkness it was impossible for a man to see the hazard unless he knew it was there, and knew where to look. To make the matter more serious, the saw was placed in such a manner that the teeth were toward the door.

Supper over, Channer left the table and started out to look after his team and bed then down for the night. As he left the comparative brightness of the cook shack for the deep night outside, he was temporarily blinded in the dark, stumbled on the step, started to fall, and threw out a hand to catch the door-post to save himself from a fall. Instead of the door-post he caught a handful of saw teeth, razor sharp, which ripped and lacerated his hand to shreds! Dripping blood in a steady stream he turned back into the room, with a few choice remarks about the fellow who put that saw there — which remarks we will discreetly delete from the present record!

Maria came running from the kitchen with a clean dish towel and a bottle of turpentine, roundly cursing the man who had left the saw there. She soused the hand with turpentine and tied it up, while Pedro went out to take care of the team. Al was advised to head for town and a doctor, but like all the tough, hardy characters, of whom he was a worthy representative, he laughed at the idea and went to bed. But sleep fled his pillow, and the next morning his hand was so stiff and sore another man had to harness and care for his team. He worked as usual up to noon, and then his hand was in such serious condition Pedro summarily ordered him out of camp and on the way to the doctor.

As Al slowly rode toward home behind his great team, he suddenly remembered that this was Thursday, the last day of the revival meetings. Like a bolt from the blue the thought struck him, "I laughed at the idea of ever getting converted, and thought that I was safe in camp until the meeting was ended. Is it possible that the hand of the Lord is in this matter, and that God allowed the accident to take place so that I might have one more chance, and not die lost?" He was in a serious mood as he rode along, and deeply distressed in his heart. He shrank from the idea of making a spectacle of himself, and while he cared little for the opinions and scoffing of most of his friends, he could not bear to think of facing Herb and his sneers.

When he drew near his home, his mother was waiting for him in the clearing. Whether it was intuition or some other form of mental telepathy known only to mothers, she had a premonition that her favourite son was on the way home in trouble. Like most frontier women, she was skilled in the rude surgery of the times, and she dressed Al's hand without saying very much. But Al knew what was in her mind, and suddenly without any preliminary introduction, he blurted out, "I could be a Christian if Herb was one!"

His mother smiled and quietly said, "Herb was saved last night!"

With those words the bottom dropped out of his opposition, and he found himself alone with God and the need to make a decision. He went to the barn and put his team away, working with one hand, and sat down to do some thinking. Then he went across to the Dass farm to talk with Bessie, to whom he already formed the habit of looking for advice and counsel. What passed between them at that momentous interview is no one else's business, but that night they sat together in the closing service of the revival meeting. When the invitation was given, Al was the first one down the aisle to confess Christ and pledge himself to live for Him. And the first person to congratulate him was his chum, Herb, the only one he feared would scoff! Incidentally, Herb also entered the ministry shortly after Al did, so that the influence and effect of that revival in the backwoods is still going on. The series of meetings had made a clean sweep of the younger element, and the partners in the dance hall were all among the converts, together with most of the community who had not been in the church before the effort was started.

For a few days Al stayed around Kelsey while his hand began to heal, studying and reading the Bible which his mother gave him after his conversion. His eager and quick mind soaked up the teachings of the Word of God as a dry sponge absorbs water, and the doctrines of grace profoundly moved and pleased him. He had long talks with the elders, who knew the Bible; especially with his godly mother, whose instruction he was eager to heed. In the back of his mind, however, was the problem of going back to Pedro's tough camp, to be laughed at, in all probability, by Pedro and the boys. He didn't mind that so much, as he could lick any three of them, but he dreaded Maria's shrewish and vile tongue, knowing he had no way to answer her blasphemies.

When he finally started back to camp, he had decided that he would have to declare himself at the start, or be false to the Lord Jesus Whom he had pledged himself to serve. He arrived in camp just before the supper hour, put his team in the rude shed, and went in to greet the boys. There was a shout of welcome, for he was popular with his fellow jacks, and they crowded around to ask about his injured hand. In the midst of the noise and chatter Pedro announced supper by banging on a piece of railroad iron, which was hung near the door, and they all trooped to the table.

Now was the time—and Al swallowed a lump, went to the head of the table, took his Bible out of his pocket, laid it on the table, and said, "Boys, before I sit down to eat I have something to say. You know me and my life, the good of it, if any, and the bad, of which there has been plenty. But this past week I went to a revival meeting in Kelsey, and I got saved. By that I mean I accepted Jesus Christ as my Lord and Master, and I aim to follow Him all the rest of my life. I'm through with the ways of sin and wildness, I am done with cursing and blaspheming God's name. I am not trying to tell you fellows how to live, I'm just telling you how *I* am going to live. If you see me reading my Bible in the camp, or catch me on my knees by the side of the bed praying, don't think I've gone crazy. It's just what a man trying to be a Christian has to do to keep himself from backsliding, and I don't intend to slide back!"

He sat down with his heart in his throat, waiting for the howl of derision he expected. But before any of the men recovered from the shock of the bold announcement, Maria, who had been listening in the kitchen door, walked over to the table and picked up the Book. She stood there for a minute ruffling the pages, then in a voice curiously gentle she said, "A Bible! That's the first one that's ever been in one of our camps, and the only one I've had in my hands since I was a very little girl. You boys wouldn't believe it to see me now as you know me, but my mother taught me a great deal out of that Book. She used to read it to her kids every night, and some of it stuck."

She put the Bible down and said in a fierce tone, "If Al wants to be a Christian, there ain't none of you dirty so and so's who is going to stop him. I've been pretty tough and hard, but from now on when Al Channer is at my table there will be no more cursing and swearing, and the first guy that tells a dirty story will get a skillet busted over his head!" Turning to her husband, she said, "And that goes for you, too, Pedro, and I mean it!" Then she wiped a hand across her eyes and fled to the kitchen to have a good cry by herself.

Al listened in dumbfounded amazement. Could this be the tough, loose-moraled woman he had known for the past months? But while he was trying to get his thoughts back into shape, Pedro came over and said, "Al, I'd like to shake hands with a boy who has guts enough to nail his flag to the mast like that! If anybody tries to turn you away from your faith, tell Pedro. He has a shotgun full of buckshot for the skunk that would try to hinder a man from being a Christian if he wants to try!"

Al never forgot the priceless lesson he learned from his first testimony, and stand. He realized that even the toughest citizens respect a man who believes, and who does not apologize for his faith. Not given to compromise in any issue, he nevertheless resolved to speak boldly for Christ whenever he had a chance to open his mouth. Night after night he lay in his hard bunk studying the Bible, and day after day he told the men some of the things he learned. The interest got so intense that finally a group came to him and rather sheepishly asked him to teach them in an informal Bible class. Al replied, "You boys know I am not a preacher. I'm just a lumberjack like you. But if you want to listen to an amateur teach the Bible, we'll have amateur Bible classes!"

So began the ministry of a man not ordained to an ecclesiastical office, but manifestly ordained of God to a great and profitable career. Nightly the men gathered in the cook shack to hear Al expound the Scriptures, and the most interested persons in the group were Pedro and Maria. The jug of bootleg liquor disappeared, the "Badger Game" was laid on the shelf with the forgotten shotgun as the Word of God found its way into these darkened hearts. Some of the more responsible men turned to Christ, and the whole atmosphere of the camp was changed.

So passed the days until Pedro's contract was finished, and the camp broke up. Maria kissed Al goodbye, wept with grief at the separation, and swore that she was going to be a different person now that she had found God again. She kept that vow to the day she died, having lived as a vital testimony to the changing power of the Bible, and to the value of the influence of one man who was not ashamed of the Gospel of Christ.

In the meantime Martin Cain had opened a camp near Kelsey, and Al found employment there as a cant-hook hand on a loading landing. This is a job that called for some considerable measure of skill as well as a great deal of brawn, but young Channer had an abundance of both. As an instance of the muscular power of the old-time jack, let me recite a typical episode in an ordinary day's work. At one time Al and a partner were teamed up together on a drive, and were separated from camp by a roaring river in flood. The two worked with pike and cant-hook to keep the logs from piling up along the bank and starting a jam. The river was full of logs hurtling along on the swift current. When darkness came and supper was announced by the familiar clang of the iron, the two men looked across the raging stream with its freight of moving timber, and wondered how they could cross to supper and their bunks. Finally Al's pal said, "Sink your hook into a log and we'll make a raft." So the two men each stabbed the point of his cant-hook into a separate log and drew the two together. Gripping the logs with the cant-hooks, they jumped on them with their calked boots, thrust out from the bank and crossed in the dark. They had only the strength of their leg muscles to hold the two logs together, the current twisted them from end to end, and hurling logs smashed into their "raft" all the way across. But they made the passage, stepped nonchalantly off their hazardous craft, and went quietly in to supper. It was just an incident in the day's work for them, and nothing to brag about!

Channer started to work for Martin Cain on a Monday morning, and when Wednesday night came he walked four miles through the dark to attend prayer meeting at Kelsey, and this after fourteen hours of labour in the woods. Then four long miles back through the dark and the weather to rest on a hard bunk before the next day dawned with its toil and danger. Each Sunday he made the same round trip, as he desired the fellowship and strength to be found only in organized worship in the house of God; be that house ever so humble.

Because Martin Cain himself loved the Gospel and had the interest of his men at heart, the atmosphere of his camps was far above the average, and the men did not scoff at the new hand who was seen reading his Bible at every possible moment, and who always knelt in prayer by the side of his bunk before he sought his pillow. In fact, they greatly admired his courage and faith, and those who did not took one look at his huge frame and decided to be discreet! In Kelsey, meanwhile, they had built the small church, and the young people had started a Christian Endeavor Society, as that great youth movement was in its hey-day at the time. Participating in the testimony meetings gave Al an ease in speaking, and testifying in camp had given him a fluent style. His "amateur" Bible classes were still going on, and he was gaining force and reputation as the days went by.

One Sunday morning he showed up for church, as was his custom, and one of the elders met him at the door. He greeted him, and said, "Al, we have no preacher this morning. The Reverend was not able to get here. We want you to take the pulpit and bring the message."

Channer said, "Wait a minute! I'm no preacher!" The elder said, "Just get up and do your best!"

So the "amateur" teacher opened his Bible and taught

the congregation out of his heart and the Scriptures, and all left profoundly moved. The next Sunday when Al went to church he asked, "Do you have a preacher yet?"

"No," said the elder, "we haven't even looked for one! We don't need a preacher while we have you."

For six weeks Channer supplied the pulpit, and of course his reputation as a preacher filtered back to the woods. One day he was sent alone to axe out some skids for a new landing. The task done, he was walking back to camp when he met the foreman. He stopped and said, "Al, we hear you are quite a preacher. You know we never have any Gospel meetings here in camp, and the boys elected me to ask you if you won't preach to *us* some time. How about it?"

Leaping at the opportunity, Al replied, "Any time you say. How about next Sunday afternoon?"

"That's all right with us," the foreman said, and the date was settled.

He had never worked in any camp where Gospel services had been held, so he was strictly "on his own." At the morning service in Kelsey he told the elders of his plans, and borrowed some hymn books from the church. Back in camp he made a pulpit out of a box, arranged the benches for seats, and got ready to conduct his initial service. Two of his brothers were in the crowd, neither of them a professing Christian. One of the men, John, was a monotone of the most distressing kind, as he had a very raucous voice and could not hear himself. Al began by stating that he intended to bring them a message from the Word of God. Then he passed out the hymn books and announced a number. They had no organ, no piano, or other musical accompaniment, so Al started the tune and the others joined in.

Brother John opened his mouth and bellowed the words in a manner that would have discouraged a flock of crows! The other men just quit and gazed at John in wonder and awe, since *nobody* could follow a tune while he was holding forth. After the meeting Al asked John, "Why in the name of common sense did you have to try to sing when you know you can't, and why did you bellow so loud?"

Perfectly seriously John replied, "Al, you are my brother and I was sorry for you, so I wanted to help you out!"

"That's nice," Al said, "but the next time you want to help me, do it by keeping your mouth shut! You conked the song service and killed it deader than a mackerel."

But the sermon had life enough in it, and the men were delighted and proud that one of their own camp jacks was a preacher of such ability. They attended his Bible class, listened earnestly to his sermons, and not a few of them turned to Christ and received salvation. When Martin Cain learned that he had a gifted preacher on his pay-roll he was delighted, and made a trip up to the camp to hear Channer preach. He encouraged the boy to keep on, and said his work was not to interfere with his ministry, which was more important than getting out timber.

The Presbytery of Duluth was then employing a minister who acted as evangelist for small rural churches, and in the course of his work he came to Kelsey to hold meetings. This man, the Rev. Franklin Barakman, was a man of deep spirit and generous heart, and when he heard Al preach he was greatly impressed. He was strongly persuaded that Al was called of God to preach to the jacks, but Al said he was not a candidate for ordination, as he lacked the necessary formal education. The preacher replied, "Some men are ordained of God who are not called of men, nor recognized by formal church authorities. God has laid His hand on you, and in His own way and time He will put you where you belong."

Being the sort of Calvinist who believes in helping God out when he could, Mr. Barakman sought out

Frank Higgins and said, "Up in a camp near Kelsey there is a young giant who is doing a great work for God. I went up there to conduct a revival, and found out I wasn't needed. This young fellow, Al Channer, a lumberjack, has set the whole region on fire, and you ought to get hold of him for your staff of camp evangelists."

So Frank sent word to Al, asking him to come to Duluth to meet with the seven men who worked for him in the camps. Frank had the authority of the Board of National Missions to engage any help he needed, but capable men were few and far between. Al had heard of Higgins but had never met him, and curiosity drew him. The conference was to meet the following week in the Duluth Y.M.C.A., and Channer made the trip. There he met John Sornberger, whose fame as an outlaw had awed him as a lad, and shook hands with Jack McCall. When the meeting began Frank introduced Al and asked him to tell of his experience. In simple words that rang with sincerity and honesty, Channer told the older men of his experiences. He detailed his own conversion, and told how he had started out to study and teach, and how he had then started to preach. He told of some of the men who had been saved in his meetings, and said, "It is a good and lucky thing I work for Martin Cain, as he backs me up in everything I want to do!"

Frank Higgins interrupted with a shout, "Praise God! You work for Martin Cain? He started *me* in this work." He ran over to Al, threw his arms around him in a bear hug and said, "Boy, throw away that cant-hook and grab a Bible. From now on you are working for me—and for God!"

So Al lost his amateur standing, and went home a full-fledged sky-pilot, commissioned as such by the incomparable Frank Higgins. His heart glowed with pride that he was accepted into the company of the spiritual giants, and he vowed he would never fail them or the Lord.

Through danger by fire, by water, by blizzard, and by pestilence he never failed, and as these words are written he is carrying on alone, the last of the giants of that era still active in the Minnesota woods. Of that subsequent career we will now read, and see the epic drama of a great life unfold.

# One Man and God, Equals Success

# CHAPTER II

# One Man and God, Equals Success

Formally employed by Frank Higgins as a camp evangelist, Al was now under the care of the Board of National Missions, and thought that his troubles were over. He envisioned the security and confidence natural to a man who had so great a church to back him, even though his salary was only fifty dollars a month. But he reckoned without the peculiar psychology of Board secretaries, and as yet knew nothing of the jealousy that sought to hinder and hamper the work of evangelism in the north woods. Frank paid him a great compliment when he turned him loose to make his own program and choose his own camps in which to work — an honour and trust which the Sky Pilot never conferred upon any other of his men. He worked in this happy fashion under Higgins for four years, until Frank met his untimely death and was succeeded by John Sornberger. All of the time, of course, he was an employee of the National Missions Committee, of whom he had a highly exalted opinion.

He had reason to revise his views to a minor extent when the end of the month rolled around. His voucher was sent in by Higgins, but no pay check arrived. This happened the second and third time, and Christmas was upon them. One other new man on Higgins' staff was in the same financial distress, a man named Bell, who was allocated the camps along the Soo Line where some thousands of men were employed. The National Missions Committee of Presbytery called a meeting with Higgins and his staff to consider a letter they had received from the Board about Channer and Bell. The dignitaries had concluded that Frank did have the authority to hire new men, but since there was no provision in the budget the Board could not pay them! Frank roared his disapproval and said, "Now I have to drop my work and go to New York to straighten this out, and the trip will cost me more than the amount involved!"

Bell said, "That means we do not get our salary?"

"Not just yet," Frank replied.

Al said with a wry smile, "That's a nice Christmas present to hand a man right out of the blue! I've heard about red tape, but this will be the first time I ever ate it for Christmas dinner!"

Elder McCabe of the Glen Avon Church session arose in great indignation and said, "We will see that these men get paid for their labours, if we have to do it out of our own pockets. This work is of God and must be supported. I will pay Mr. Channer the three months due him, and one of my friends will pay Mr. Bell. Tell the Board that if they will not pay Frank's men, the Glen Avon Church will, and deduct the amount from its benevolence funds, paying them directly!" When this news reached the Board, they changed their decision in a hurry, since Glen Avon was a comparatively wealthy church and its benevolence contribution was a heavy one.

Bell quit in disgust, saying he wouldn't work for a bunch like that, one that would leave a man stranded for Christmas!" But Al was made of sterner stuff. At the time of this writing he had finished thirty-five years as a missionary under the Board, and is still going strong. The men who are in closest touch with the work of the evangelism in the north woods are constantly puzzled by the manner in which this field is treated from the New York office. An appropriate text for them would be, "Blindness hath happened in part to this people!" Quite recently the Board tried to move Channer out of his parish, where he is the only missionary-evangelist in sixty-seven thousand square miles, and send him to Alaska! This would have left the entire area without one missionary, silenced the voice of the Gospel in the logging camps, and blacked out completely the effort which has been made at a cost of money and labour for so many years. And only the firm and unyielding stand of the Session of the First Church in Duluth prevented the shift being made!

When John Sornberger laid down his labours and departed to be with the Lord, he knew that Al was the only and rightful successor. He called him in for a talk and said, "Al, your chief cross will be the fact that men who live two thousand miles away, who never saw a lumber camp or a lumberjack, who know nothing about the bitter lot of the pioneer people of the border, will handicap and hamstring you at every turn. Instead of letting a man who knows the country and the people do the job, they'll pester you with fool ideas and weigh you down with red tape until you won't be able to move! They've had their harpoon in me for thirty-five years, and when I shake it loose they'll sink it in you! You will not only have to fight sin and the devil, you'll also have to battle the 'big shots' who ought to be your best friends!"

The present executive of the Board of National Missions, who has the duty of administering this field is Dr. Earl Jackman, and he is a man of vision. He is a true friend to the project of evangelizing the frontiers, and is the type of Christian and missionary statesman who can see the value of this work so, as this record is written, the missionaries of this great region work under the supervision of one who is sympathetic and understanding, and kindly in his approaches to the unique problems which are daily presented. Al Channer has often expressed to the writer his great esteem for Dr. Jackman, and his happiness and pleasure in working with him. It is certainly a great change from previous days, and one vastly appreciated. May he long continue in this strategic office!

From the beginning of his work under Higgins, it was evident that Channer had found his rightful place of service, and he was a success from the start. He had a jolly manner, a warm affection for men he worked with, and a natural charm which made friends for him from the first meeting. Grand opera did not lose anything when he entered the ministry, but he had a pleasing voice and could lead a song service to the satisfaction of the men, when he was not handicapped by his brother John. Camp after camp received him gladly, and he left a train of redeemed lives behind him as he passed along. Welcomed at first because he was one of Higgins' men, he soon won the right to go where he desired to because he was Channer, and the jacks had come to admire and respect him. He shared their bunks, he ate their meals with them, when help was needed he grabbed an axe, a cant-hook, or a peavey and was one of them. But when the day was ended, and he stood up in the camp to open his Bible and preach Christ to them, he was God's man, called of the Spirit and manifestly under His unction.

To show the attitude of these tough old timers to the Gospel, two incidents will be sufficient illustration. Channer went on one occasion to a new camp he had never entered before, which was operated by the Kline Company. When he entered the camp building, he saw the storekeeper talking to an itinerant jewelry salesman; one of the hardy souls who roamed the woods selling cheap watches and such articles as a jack might be induced to buy. Al stood aside to wait until the salesman had finished, and while waiting the door banged open and the foreman stormed in. At the first glance Al recognized him as a famous "Bull of the Woods," named Cordy. He was reputed to be one of the toughest characters in the north.

He had lost one eye in a rough-house, his face was scarred all over from the calk marks left when his enemies had put the boots to him, and he had a cauliflower ear draped on one side of his head. When he saw the two strangers, Cordy snarled, "What the —— are you two doing in my camp? Got a permit from the company to come on this property?"

While the salesman hastily reached for his credentials to display them to the belligerent foreman, Al quietly slipped out the door. He had no permit, and never did carry one. His Bible was the only credential he had: that, and his personal reputation. As he passed through the door the supper horn blew, and Al streaked for the cook shack. He ate in a hurry, so that he was almost through when the foreman came in, still in a black mood. As soon as the foreman had bolted his meal and went out, Al followed and accosted him. "Mr. Cordy," he said, "I am a minister of the Gospel, a Sky Pilot. I came here to hold services for your men, but I do not have a permit. I guess I could get one, but I didn't think to do so."

Cordy interrupted him to say, "A preacher, huh? Do you preach the Gospel?"

Al said, "Brother, that's all I know!"

Cordy said, "Then you don't need no permit. My camp is open to you, Reverend. Can we have services tonight?"

Al said, "Yes, sir! That's what I am here for!"

Cordy nodded and passed on.

A half hour later Al entered the bunk-house, where the jewelry salesman was displaying his wares to the interested men. He sat back to wait until the salesman finished, and while he waited the door swung open and the foreman strode in. He gave a glance around the bunk-house, spotted Channer and growled, "I thought there was going to be a meeting here!"

"There is," Al assured him, "as soon as this salesman is finished. I don't think it would be courteous to interrupt him."

Cordy rasped, "To —— with him and his junk. You preach! That's important!"

He dragged a box to the center of the room and said, "Men, we have a Sky Pilot here, and he's going to preach to us. This is a church service, and I want order. Any son that makes a disturbance or bothers this meeting will have me on him, and I'll stomp the living daylights out of him!"

The men roared at the dignified introduction, and gathered around to listen. Under the circumstances Al didn't want to spend time on a song service, so he just opened his Bible, read the Scripture, and started to preach. He was naturally on his mettle, and he knew of Cordy's reputation as a desperate and hardened bully, and he tried to reach the man. Cordy listened in profound interest and deep attention, and when the meeting closed with prayer he rose and said, "Preacher, you're all right, and them's true words you spoke." He shook hands and said, "Any of my camps are open to you day or night, and you'll be welcome whenever you show up." Then he turned and went out into the night.

Al followed him, and said, "Mr. Cordy, I'd like a further word with you. I know you are not a Christian, why don't you take Christ and be saved?"

Very earnestly the foreman said, "Channer, I'd like to, but I've got a job to do, and to get out timber you have to be tough. Later on I want to talk more about this, but not now. Some other time." With that the two separated.

"Some other time," never came for Cordy, as is so often the case with others. Three weeks later he was on a flying trip to Duluth, and one dark night his enemies caught up with him and beat him to death. It must have been an epic battle that raged in the dark by the side of a byway in Lester Park, but the story was never disclosed. His body was found the next morning, broken and bruised, and his murderers were never apprehended. He died as he had lived, tough, hard, swinging with both hands and asking no quarter. But tough as he was he reverenced the Gospel and respected the preacher, and his attitude was typical of his entire tribe.

One night Al Channer came into a camp to hold a meeting, arriving just in time for supper. It had been a nasty, cold, drizzling day, and most of the men were wet through. Supper over, the jacks hurried to their bunk-house; in this case, the old-fashioned "muzzle-loader" type of building. More than a hundred men were crowded in the one single room. Two huge barrel stoves glowed red-hot in the center of the room, surrounded by the wet, steaming woolen clothes of the men. The odor of sweat swept up from unwashed bodies in waves that were almost visible, to join their fragrance to that of steaming wool and drying socks. The men were practically all smoking and spitting on the hot stove, to raise small bursts of steam to help the air, which could have been cut with an axe.

When the preacher entered the closed room, it hit him like a blow in the face. He worked his way down through the crowd until he reached the rear end, where the ubiquitous grindstone stood. He piled his hymn books on the end of the frame and faced the men. There was an unwritten law in the camps that a door could not be opened, as night air might be fatal. Al tried to take a breath and couldn't. There wasn't a breath left to take.

He raised his voice and said, "Boys, we are about to have a meeting, but before we begin I want to make a suggestion. I realize it is cold outside and you boys came in wet, and you don't realize how bad this air is. But I just came in from the open, and I want to tell you that between the drying clothes and the socks that never saw a cake of soap, and the pipe smoke, the stench is just awful. Let us have the door open until the meeting is over."

There was a tall, lanky jack coiled up on a bench. He rose and went to the one huge door, he swung it open, and went back to his bench and settled down. But he was no more than settled before some fellow slyly banged the door shut. It shook the building, and the tall boy turned his head and surveyed the group by the door. Slowly he uncoiled himself again, length by length, until the whole six and a half feet of him were upright. Without a word he plodded to the door and opened it again. Back he went to his seat and coiled down.

Bang! went the door, practically in tune with the arrival of the seat of the huge man's trousers on the bench. Once again the big jack unfolded himself and started for the door. Once again he opened it, and turned back to his seat. He started to sit down, then spun around just in time to catch the culprit in the act of slamming the door shut. With two swift strides he had the offender by the collar of his shirt and was wrestling him around while the smaller man fought like a wild-cat. Then the tall man got a grip on the trouser leg of his opponent with his other hand, and swung him clear of the floor. With a mighty heave he tossed him ten feet through the air. The victim landed on a bunk with such force that his feet hit the wall so hard the whole building shook. Not a word had been spoken, and the song service was going on without interruption as the men in front bellowed the tune. The tall man went back and sat down, and the meeting went on to its close. When the benediction was pronounced, the big man came up to shake hands with the preacher, and he said, "Well, Bud, I kept the door open! If the preacher wants air, air is what he is going to get." Without a smile he turned and walked away.

That attitude of mind was characteristic. Whatever the Sky Pilot wanted he could have, if the camp could provide it. When a heckler appeared, the other boys gave him a rough and short shift. The cook always had the choicest morsels for the preacher when he appeared, and any man was proud to share his bed–and his bugs!–with the man of God. This wholesome affection came partly because of their innate respect for the Gospel, partly because of the childhood training from which no person ever entirely escapes, and partly out of admiration for the sheer manhood of these stalwart missionaries, who earned their way as far as they went.

These camps were the refuge and hiding places of wanted men, for the arm of the law, long as it is reputed to be, was too short to reach as far back as the timber extended. One day Channer saw a load coming down a skid-way in one of the camps deep in the woods, and he thought that the black horses and the brown logs against the white snow would make a good picture. He got his camera ready, and when the team got close he stepped out and said to the driver, "Just a minute, Bud." The man looked up and saw a camera pointed at him. He leaped off the load and ran like a rabbit! His picture was in every rogues' gallery in the country, and he was naturally a little camera shy!

At one time it was standard practice for a sheriff who wanted a man out of the camps to come to the edge of a clearing, call the foreman, and tell him who he was after. The foreman would then announce that a sheriff was in camp, and a third of the crew would take to the brush until the peace officer was safely away! But even the roughest and rudest of them had childhood memories and respected the preacher, even though they did not accept and obey his preachments.

All of these Sky Pilots were hardy men, and walked with danger as a matter of course. Close calls and hazardous happenings were their common fare, and they took them in their stride. On one certain occasion Channer had to make a trip back into the camps in the attempt to bring out a very sick man to the hospital, and a blizzard was raging when he started. He had chains on all four wheels, the cars of that day had such high clearance he thought he had a 50-50 chance to make it, and none of these warriors ever asked better odds than that. As he drove up the North Shore the wind howled against the curtains of his car, the snow seeped in, and the road was all but lost in the white waste.

When he was past Two Harbors, he found the road which went back into the timber, and turned right into the teeth of the wind. A fifty mile an hour gale hurtled against his windshield, and he could hardly keep the car on the road. The only way he could be sure he was on the road was by watching the fence posts on either side, and keeping half way between them. It was while watching these fences that he noticed a side road and a mail box, a circumstance which was to save his life.

A quarter of a mile farther on his car quit dead. He got out, struggled with the wind as he fought to get the hood up, and found that his motor was frozen into a solid block of ice. The snow had blown in through the radiator and frozen all over the motor.

In desperation he turned to his cold car, then remembered the mail box he had seen a short way back. He turned, and now on foot fought his way step by step through the storm. His eyes were blinded by snow, icicles formed on his face, and he was blue with cold and numb beyond feeling. As he staggered along, providentially the wind lulled for a few seconds, and he saw a narrow plank bridge spanning a ditch by the side of the road. He thought, "That must lead to a house," and turned across to follow it. Just before he lost consciousness he reached a porch, and fell full length.

A man came to the door, exclaiming in surprise, and dragged him into a warm and lighted room. Al dimly heard a woman say, "Why, it's Reverend Channer! What on earth is *he* doing out in a storm like this?"

When he woke up he was in a warm bed, wrapped in woolen blankets, and had suffered no harm that a good rest and plenty of hot soup would not cure. His rescuers were members of the First Presbyterian Church of Duluth, and had recognized the renowned camp preacher in spite of his frosted coating! But if it had not been for the sudden lull of the storm at just the exact instant, the preacher would have staggered on past the one refuge in all the frozen waste, to perish in a drift of snow.

Like all of these giants, Channer was a capable evangelist almost from the start. The meetings he has held, and the opposition he has overcome would make a volume of fascinating stories. It was the custom for the Sky Pilot to take a local pastor into the camps with him from time to time, especially one who had the masculinity to appeal to the jacks. There was a stalwart Methodist pastor at Virginia named Norleman, who became acquainted with Al and expressed a desire to make such a trip. He was delighted with the experience, and was deeply moved by the reverent manner in which the men listened to the message.

When they returned to Virginia, the pastor said, "Al, we ought to do something like that for the men in the mill here in town." Al agreed, and promised to try. At that time the Virginia Mill was the largest one in the north and employed a great force of men. With the consent of the company, Channer set out to find a time when the men could listen, and discovered that the lunch period at night was the only available hour. The day shift went home to eat at noon, but the night crew brought their lunches and ate at the mill. So Channer and the pastor came one night at midnight to try a new experiment in evangelism. Nearly two hundred men came to the service and listened with interest and pleasure, which started the wheels rolling. For six months the midnight meetings continued, since the crews alternated, working days one week and nights the next. This brought them all under the sound of the Gospel, and a revival broke out among them which spread to their homes. At the end of the six months Pastor Norleman was transferred to Cambridge, Wisconsin, and since Al was away up in the Rainy River region, the meetings closed.

When Dr. Norleman arrived in Cambridge, he became pastor of the oldest Norwegian Methodist Church in America, but there was little else to recommend the town or the situation. There had been no revival or evangelistic services in Cambridge for over forty years, and the leaders of the religious community were unanimous in their opinion that such would be impossible. They had completely surrendered any hope of revival. The pastor of the Presbyterian Church, the Rev. Schuster, did not share the general pessimism, but his church was dominated by the leading elder, and his hands were tied. This elder was the local leader. He was mayor of the city, president of the Commercial Club, and the social dictator. But he was completely indifferent to the progress of the Gospel or the salvation of men.

When the two pastors met and became acquainted, they discovered a mutual desire for a quickening of the religious life of the city, and found that they shared a conviction that a revival was possible, in spite of the pessimism of the old timers. They began to lay plans, and after some weeks they presented their desire to their two congregations. The Methodist stewards voted to give their pastor full authority to do as he felt wisest, but the Presbyterian minister ran into opposition. His dominant elder was against any effort which he called "sensationalism," and only consented when the rest of the Session voted him down. Then he proposed certain conditions which he felt would safeguard his position. They were:

The revival must be led by a Presbyterian minister.

They would have one week of meetings in each of the two churches.

The meeting each night would last just sixty minutes.

There would be no "altar call" or invitation given at any service.

The Methodist pastor said he would consent to the

arrangement if he could pick the Presbyterian preacher, and he was given the authority to proceed.

Without telling him of the conditions, Channer was invited, and accepted. He did not know he was to wear spiritual handcuffs and drag a religious ball and chain until he arrived, and his friend broke the news to him. Al felt he was too far in to withdraw, so he decided to try. He had been widely advertised, billed as "The Sky Pilot," and since many had heard of him there was great interest. They had planned to begin in the Presbyterian Church the first week, running from Sunday morning through Friday night. Al was warned that if the service lasted more than an hour, half of his audience would walk out and leave him. He smiled and said, "I'm used to that. It will be quite an experience to have half of the crowd stay through one of my sermons!"

They got off to a good start. Al preached so long the first morning the meeting lasted an hour and a half, and nobody moved. The crowd was almost doubled Sunday night, and great interest was aroused in this unique preacher, who handled sin as he would twist a log with a cant-hook. By Friday night things were so warm the mayor could hold out no longer, and came to find the church so full he could hardly get in. He had to sit right on the front seat, to his distress. As the singing went on and the testimonies were given he began to fidget. He worked his way to the back, took a chair into a side room where he could hide behind a door, and composed himself to listen.

The crowd was deeply moved by Channer's message, as he blasted sin, warned of its consequences, and tenderly portrayed the love of God as it was manifested in the Cross of Christ. When he reached the end, he closed by saying, "Most of you know the conditions which were imposed on me at the start of this meeting, and that I am under promise not to give an altar call. So I will not give an invitation. I will only do this." He picked up a chair and turned it around so the back faced him, and continued, "But if any needy sinner in this audience wants to accept Christ, let him come and kneel at this chair, and all the politicians and powers in the universe will not be able to keep him out of the Kingdom of God."

Immediately a woman rose from her place, came down to the front and knelt at the chair, quietly weeping. Al placed another chair by the side of the first one and said, "Here is room for one more." This time a man came and knelt saying, "I want to take Jesus Christ as my Saviour, preacher, please pray for me!" Al merely said, "God bless you, my friend," and placed another chair. He said no further word, but just placed chair after chair until the front of the church was filled with weeping penitents!

The mayor left the meeting in a huff, saying that Al had broken the agreement by giving an invitation and demanding that the meetings close. The Presbyterian pastor stood his ground and said that Channer had not given an altar call. The people who came did so because their own hearts and desires brought them. The obdurate elder stormed at the pastor, and demanded that he call off further participation in the meeting or take the consequences. With great dignity the minister replied that the mayor might run the town and even dominate the church, but he himself was working for God, and would leave his case and his interest in His hands. He finished by saying, "As for you, my brother, let me speak a word of warning. This spirit of revival which is beginning to sweep our city is of God, and be careful that you are not found fighting Him!" The mayor replied that he would take his chances, and left.

Sunday morning the meetings moved to the Methodist Church, and Al was turned loose with no strings on him or his message. The crowds overflowed the building every night, and at the close of each message an altar call was given and scores were saved. As to the enduring nature of the stand taken by the converts, it is good to count the number of them who afterward entered the ministry, and are still preaching today. The interest was already at white heat in the middle of the week, when news came that the mayor, the only opposing force in the community, had been stricken with some sudden illness. The doctors could not diagnose his ailment, and he was rushed to the hospital in Madison. The following day the Methodist preacher went over to see him, and was told that he was in a coma and could have no visitors. He asked the nurse what was wrong with the patient, and the nurse replied, "Frankly, we don't know. It seems to be some sort of stroke. And another puzzling thing we can't figure out. He lies there, barely conscious, moaning over and over, 'My God! The Pilot!' Do you know what Pilot he means?"

"Yes!" the preacher answered, "he means the *Sky* Pilot!" and he turned away in sadness of heart and left.

The mayor died the next day without regaining consciousness, and that pulled the plug. Like the waters of a spring freshet the spirit of repentance and contrition swept the city, and the resulting meeting will be remembered as long as the participants live. Al left the town shaken out of its indifference, on fire with zeal for God, and fervor for the Gospel. Its churches were crowded to the doors for many months to come. As a result his fame grew, and he was in constant demand for evangelistic campaigns all over the north. But his heart was in the lumber camps with the jacks, and he turned his back on outside work to bury himself again in the timber with the boys who were his especial love and particular charge.

The favor of God rested upon the small but hardy band of giants, and every camp in the north sought their services. The whisky peddlers fought them ruthlessly, and the harpies who preyed on the payroll of the lumber camps tried repeatedly to get bullies to drive the Sky Pilots out of the territory, but none of these preachers had ever learned to run! And when word reached the jacks that the sinful were trying to run out these preachers, the boys organized an informal but widespread vigilance committee. They served notice to all and sundry that if harm came to any of Higgins' men, the jacks would quit work and hunt the perpetrators like wolves, to string every person concerned to the nearest tree, and the highest limb! The warning sufficed, for the saloon keepers and gamblers had seen rioting woodsmen tear up too many towns by the roots and throw the pieces away, and they wanted no part of that with themselves on the receiving end! Thus, surrounded by those who hated them, guarded by those who loved them, the shanty-man preachers went their stormy way. They waded through snow, they forded flooded streams, they toured the camps on snowshoes, skis, foot, and by dog sled and canoe, and in their wake they spread salvation and brought light and life to men. There is an impressive list of homes reunited and families made happy by the return of a prodigal husband and father, and the parents who got their sons back cleansed in spirit and decent in conduct constitute so great a company no man can number them. The preaching of the Cross may be foolishness to those who perish, but to such as hear it and heed it, the message brings new life and true happiness. And all of these men had the one theme, "Jesus Saves!"

Up to his ears in the camp ministry, Al heard that Higgins had been stricken and taken to the hospital for an operation. A cloud of sorrow and sympathy threw a shadow over their work, but the men redoubled their efforts and carried on for Frank. He sent many messages to them from the hospital, and all of the sick man's concern was for the men of his staff and for the continuation of the work he loved. The loyalty of his group of Sky Pilots knew no bounds, and they felt that they had to do his share as well as their own. So they laboured and struggled until the day that Frank died, and their organization fell to pieces because it had no leader.

After the death of Higgins, the Presbytery of Duluth appointed John Sornberger to succeed Frank. Al Channer and Martin Johnson stayed on under Presbytery's care to assist him in the work. The wiser men of the presbytery had kept their eyes on Al, and they knew that God had marked him for great things. Some of his advisors insisted that he must be ordained, but Al was quite indifferent to the idea. He was doing all that three men should have been doing, and accomplishing more than ten average preachers could do if they all worked together. His tremendous strength carried him through crises which would have killed an average man. He laughed at hardship and revelled in opposition.

But he was anything but obstinate, and took the advice of Dr. Robert Yost, then pastor of the First Church in Duluth, and of his loyal and faithful friend, Elder Luke Marvin. They laid out a course of study for him, which he pursued under the guidance of the presbytery. His quick mind and eager desire to learn, coupled with a phenomenal memory, carried him ahead at so rapid a pace he was ordained three years later.

When Dr. Yost presented his protegé as a candidate for ordination, he made a short but compelling speech. He said, "Fathers and brethren, you and I will long remember with some embarrassment how Frank Higgins, a man approved of God, came before this presbytery year after year seeking ordination. Time after time he was rejected and refused because he did not have a formal education and possessed no degrees. In the end wiser counsel prevailed and we ordained him, and we have boasted of this action ever since!

"Now we have before us, seeking this same dignity, a man who is manifestly ordained by the Holy Spirit. The signal blessing of God has rested upon him in these early

217

A Frontier Congregation

A Lumber Jack Who Found Christ

Al Channer in Camp

Al Channer and a Congregation

years of his ministry, and he has done and is doing a work which any one of us would be proud to accomplish, but which none of us are capable of performing. Shall we honour ourselves by ordaining him, or shall we refuse to recognize the signature of God upon his natural credentials? No college or seminary in all this broad land can produce a scholar who speaks the language of the lumberjacks, nor train a man to do the work which Al Channer is so magnificently performing. All we are called to do is to formally recognize this and give him the authority to administer the sacraments, this being the only part of a minister's duties he is not already discharging. Al Channer now works under a divine commission, he is a representative of presbytery, the men he has led to Christ are legion, and the lives he has helped to reclaim are almost unnumbered, so I move that this presbytery acknowledge this great and godly man by ordaining him to the ministry."

A score of voices seconded the motion, it was unanimously carried, and the lumberjack preacher became an ordained minister, with all the rights, privileges, and powers of that position. But he left the service of ordination just as he entered it, a man who knew his calling, intended to fulfill his destiny, and who had a profound indifference to honours and titles, as long as he was free to preach the Gospel to men who were lost in sin, and had no hope aside from Jesus Christ. He was still a Sky Pilot, a jack who had been saved by grace, and as long as breath was in his body he could live only to proclaim redemption to the boys he knew and loved.

# The Tale That Is Not Ended

# CHAPTER III

# The Tale That Is Not Ended

The calling of a Sky Pilot is a peculiar one, and not one ordained minister in thousands had the many qualities which are requisite to success in this exacting field. The camp evangelist must have tremendous physical strength to bear the hardships which are a natural part of the life, and that is probably why God never called any pygmies into this service. He must know the life intimately, and be able to speak the language of the camps. He has to have a hardy and serene spirit, as waves of vulgarity, blasphemy, and bad language are apt to roll over him as the men converse in lurid phrases. He needs deep resources of the spirit, as he stands alone most of the time. And above all he must possess courage which makes him a stranger to fear. The opposition he meets may take the form of physical violence, and his life is threatened again and again.

The success of Channer's work in the woods of Minnesota was told abroad, and the Synod of Michigan asked the Presbytery of Duluth to lend their great preacher to Michigan, so he could organize such a mission in their territory. Al went to look the situation over, and found a different condition than the one he was accustomed to. The work on the peninsula was being done by imported labour of the "hill-billy" type, which had been brought in to work the cut-over lands, salvaging pine timber to be used in the production of resinous products. The reduction plant was at Antrim, Michigan, and the camps were scattered all through the stump lands.

They were bleak and somber places, having none of the charm and beauty of a true logging region. There were no stately stands of tall trees to delight the eye, no music to charm the ear as when the wind is sighing through the pines. The dwellings were crude board shacks totally lacking in any sanitary conveniences, and there was no incentive to decency of living. The people were utterly despondent and indifferent, and Antrim itself was a moral cesspool. The decent people such as the company officials, with their families, lived in the thriving and prosperous city of Mancelona a mile down the road from Antrim. The two towns had nothing in common, and the people of one were as different from the other as would be dwellers on separate planets.

Many years before the itinerant labourers had been brought up from the south, the Methodist denomination had built a church at Antrim,, and maintained a pastor there. But that was in the earlier logging days, and the members had long since moved away. The church was boarded up, deserted, abandoned, and no minister ever visited the region except on the rare occasion when one was called in for a funeral. As for weddings, the dissolute citizens did not bother with that formality, they just dwelt together and swapped mates as the fancy dictated or circumstances ruled it convenient. Utter promiscuity was the rule among the shifting population of labourers in the shattered woods and the reducing plant.

A godly Methodist woman struggled to maintain a vestigial Sunday School where a few parents allowed their youngsters to attend, chiefly to get them out of the way for an hour or two.

She and her religious ideas were tolerated; no more, and she had long abandoned any hope of ever reaching any of the adults with a plea for decency of living or moral advancement. Antrim being the center of the project, when Al came to essay the organization of camp evangelism under such circumstances, he made the wild and vile town his headquarters.

From camp to camp he went, attempting to attract some of the men to the services he held, and to win them to Christ and a better way of life. A lesser man would have quit in thirty days, but defeat is a word Channer never learned to recognize or pronounce, and he plugged away all winter. Tirelessly he trudged from camp to camp preaching, praying, carrying drunks to their bunks, binding up their wounds and fighting their battles for them. In time the men came to realize that they had a true friend in the newcomer, and some began to listen to his earnest words. A few accepted Christ, and their homes became oases of decency in the desert of sin. Some of the wives began to tell how different their men were since the Gospel had come among them, and the little Sunday School began to grow until it seemed about to burst its seams. A few of the better men began to take off their hats when they saw God's man coming, and they addressed him as "Reverend" in tones of respect and affection. It was the old story of the cleansing of Augean stables, and it took a giant to do it—a veritable spiritual Hercules.

When the winter was past and the effects of months of hard work began to show, the pastor at Mancelona, greatly encouraged, came to Al and said, "Long ago I wrote Antrim off as a place as hopeless as Sodom or Gomorrah, but I have seen a miracle performed before my eyes, and I am ready to say that with God nothing is impossible. You have transformed some of the camps, men and women have turned to God, and I thank Him daily that He sent so great a man to help us. But with all of the progress made in the camps, Antrim still remains a sink of iniquity. Brother Channer, if we open and clean up the Methodist Church there, do you have the courage and faith to try to hold a revival meeting there? All I can do is hold your hat while you fight, but I'll be at your side or your back every inch of the way. You will have the help and prayers of every decent person on the Michigan Peninsula if you make the effort, and no one will blame you if you fail."

In the several camps where Channer had been working, there was just one man of authority who was a Christian, and that was the foreman of the camp at Downey. When Al approached him he said, "Preacher, go to it! I'll be with you all the way, and I'll have a body-guard with pick handles ready to protect you at any time, and I guess you will need them!" Thus encouraged, Channer decided to venture, knowing that the success or failure of the meetings meant the beginning of better days or the end of his efforts.

The services were announced by word of mouth, and the starting date set. No time was decided upon for the close of the meetings, as the Sky Pilot was determined to carry on for as long as it took to get a break and win the day. A howl of protest went up from the whisky peddlers and the dive keepers, who wanted no interference with their traffic. The rougher element flatly stated they would break up the attempt if they had to kill the preacher to do it. Corpses were no novelty in that wild setting, and as far as I have ever heard, no murderer was ever brought to justice for one of the frequent killings. "Death by misadventure" was the stock phrase of the coroner, and the words, "Killed by a party or parties unknown" closed the career of many a friendless man who met his end by knife thrust, pistol ball, or bludgeon. Nobody with any sense would have dreamed of invading that lion's den— but the Sky Pilots did not claim to have sense! They just had great hearts that did not know the meaning of fear, and spirits that believed God could still raise the walking dead who were in the deep sleep of sin.

Al's approach was anything but diplomatic. He hurled

his defiance right in the teeth of the crowd the first night. The building was packed for the opening service, as the crowd wanted to see the man who had the temerity to walk in where angels would not like to tread, and they expected fireworks from the ultra-ungodly. His first sermon was on the commandment, "Thou shalt not commit adultery," and he closed his plain and sharp denunciation by pointing his finger at each man in turn and sternly demanding, "Whose wife are *you* with, tonight?"

The sermon made a stir, half of the crowd went away frankly admiring the sheer grit of the heroic preacher, the other half offering odds that he wouldn't live out the week. When Al entered his pulpit the second night, the church was packed and jammed. On the sacred desk was an unsigned note which said, "If you attempt to preach tonight you will be shot as you stand in the pulpit. Take warning, and get out while you can."

Al read the note aloud to the listening audience, and paused until the silence was painful. Then he threw back his head and laughed, saying, "Will somebody please open the windows? When I am shot I want to see the face of the dirty coward who would shoot an unarmed man." Then he opened his Bible and began his sermon.

The revival lasted three weeks, and in that time seventy-six of the toughest characters in the town were converted. These men proved their salvation by the immediate change made in the manner of their living. They smashed their whisky bottles, threw away their crooked dice, and went back to their own wives and families. In the middle of the first week Al started a prayer meeting in the afternoons, when women and men who worked the night shift could come for a message, and to pray for the success of the services. One woman who came asked the preacher, "Have you seen John, yet?"

"John who?" asked the evangelist.

"No, you haven't met him," said the woman, "or you

wouldn't say 'John who.' You'll know you have met him when you see him!"

His curiosity aroused, Channer asked some of his friends who the mysterious John was. They shook their heads and said, "Just pray that he stays away, because he'll break up the meeting when he gets around to it. He is a huge man, and the bully of the town. He walks the streets trying to start fights, but everybody is afraid of him. He is a ruthless bruiser, and has crippled half the men he has fought. The rest saved themselves by running when they had enough. He is a brute, and desperately cruel. If you see him, run!"

Al said, "I can't run. My feet hurt!" and laughed off the warning.

Three nights later "John" came into the meeting when it was well under way. The preacher recognized him from his description, supposed he was there for trouble and got ready to meet it. The pride of the town was the small choir of little girls who sang every night, under the direction of the lay worker who had been conducting the struggling Sunday School. They really were a lovely sight, like lilies growing in a morass. They all dressed in white, all had long curls carefully tended for the evening meeting, and they rose to sing just as the dreaded bully entered the church. To the surprise of Channer, the smallest of the lassies and one of the prettiest, waved her hand at the scowling man and cried out, "Hullo, daddy! Listen to me sing!"

The crowd chuckled with enjoyment, and Big John sank into the nearest seat, as the careful occupant hastily vacated it. He believed in "safety first," although that phrase had not been popularized. As soon as the song was ended, Al got up, read his text and preached his sermon. When he finished he gave an altar call, and some half dozen men and women responded. While he was dealing with these inquirers, the evangelist saw the smallest member of his junior choir leave her seat on the platform, run down the aisle, and climb up in the lap of the dreaded basher. The rough man cuddled her, and she put her arms around his neck, whispering in his ear for a moment. He shook his head, set her on the floor and left the church.

After the benediction Al went to the little lassie and asked, "Sweetheart, what did you say to your Daddy when you sat in his lap?"

The child replied, "I said, 'Daddy, won't you love Jesus, too? I love Him so and I love you so, and He loves you. Now won't *you* love Him?' "

The preacher put his hand on the fair head of the tiny evangelist and said, "Your Daddy *will* love Jesus some day, and don't you ever stop praying for him until he does!"

The next night Big John was back again, and he sat in the same seat. He paid close attention to the service, and seemed much impressed as it gained momentum. When Channer had finished his sermon he stated, "I am going to give an altar call again tonight, and open the doors of the Kingdom of God to any who want to enter in. Many of you here tonight know that you are sinners, and on your way to Hell. But Christ died for your sins, God is working here, and we have already seen His power in these meetings. Those of you who desire to escape Hell and find forgiveness for your sins come forward when I give the call, and accept Christ as your Saviour and Lord."

Here he was interrupted by Big John, who leaped to his feet as though he had been spurred. He started down the aisle, and half way to the front he fell on his hands and knees as though he had been hit on the head with a club. He did not try to come erect to his feet again, but *crawled* to the altar, crying on God to save him. His little daughter began to dance and leap and clap her hands, crying, "Oh, Daddy! I *knew* you would love Jesus if you would just let yourself!"

Al ran down the aisle to the troubled man, put his arms

around him, and helped him to the altar, where he found Christ, forgiveness, and peace. The next day Big John was at the prayer meeting asking for a Bible. He began to give his testimony, and when the meetings closed, John proposed that the prayer meetings continue. When he was asked, "Who will lead them?" he replied, "I will!" And he did for many, many weeks. Three months after he was saved, Big John was leading such a meeting, and he said, "I don't have to argue with the men of this town about salvation, or to prove I am saved. Everybody *knows* I am. I haven't smashed one of you fellows in the nose for three months!" They all agreed that was a miracle, and proof conclusive that a work of grace had been wrought!

The great revival at Antrim climaxed Al's work in Michigan, and left an inspired company of aroused and converted men to carry on a permanent work which lasted as long as the camps in that region functioned. The Sky Pilot had entered into the Michigan adventure with serious handicaps which would have put an ordinary man in the hospital for a long stay. The great fire of 1918 had trapped him near Kelsey, and after he had all but exhausted himself in the work of rescue, and when all the settlers had fled, he made his way to his homestead to see what he could do to salvage some of his few possessions. His family had left and he was alone. The fire was so close he could not set a back-fire to protect his home, and since it was a crown blaze, leaping a quarter of a mile at a jump, there was no reason to believe that a back-fire would do any good. He had already accepted the call to go to Michigan for the Synod's experiment, and he carried his bags to the center of the clearing. He expected the house to go in a hurry, since the underbrush and dead grass extended from the woods to his fence.

Trying to safeguard his possessions he worked a few minutes too long, and the fire had him trapped on all sides. He resigned himself as lost, but one of the many freak occurrences of that great holocaust saved him. For no earthly cause which reason could assign, the fire leaped his clearing, spared his house, and rushed on to destroy hundreds of square miles of homes and timber as it roared on its way. It claimed plenty of other men as its victims, but spared the man of God. Only a Christian could offer an explanation of this amazing escape, the natural man cannot comprehend how the hand of God is ever over those who love and serve Him, to be their defense until their work for Him is done. You will recall how snow fell before the ashes were cool, that pneumonia and "flu" came in its wake, and suffering was intense and general.

When he was assured that his family were safe, Al went on to Michigan, so exhausted he could hardly stand unaided. You would think that *any* man of flesh and blood would stop now for a rest, but the giants are made of different stuff. His throat so raw with smoke and ashes he could hardly whisper, his body so tired he was asleep on his feet, Al started for Michigan. The reason? He had promised to go, they were expecting him, and that ended the matter!

When he arrived at Mancelona, the "flu" possessed the land. Every cabin and house had someone in it sick unto death. The governor had closed the region, and had forbidden any public gatherings—even for funerals. Al went from cabin to cabin, visiting the sick and the dying, and praying with all who were alive enough to know what they were doing. In one cabin he found a woman so sick she could not rise, and a child of six months lying next to her. They were alone, and Al did what he could to make them comfortable. He learned that the mother had flu and the baby had diphtheria, and no doctor available. When he had ministered to their physical needs, he put his hands on the babe and prayed that God would spare its life.

As he went out the door he reeled and grabbed the post to hold himself until the world stopped spinning about him. He had reached the end of his strength. He rested a while, then started on the long, weary walk back to the place where he had arranged to spend the night. As he passed through Crossett he encountered a squawman, whom nobody could tolerate. This poor outcast had been a minister of the Gospel in his younger days, but drink had defeated him. He took to the woods and married an Indian squaw, forfeiting all rights to the respect of his fellow men.

When he saw that Channer was a stranger, he asked hopefully, "Are you a doctor?"

"No," Al replied, "I am a Presbyterian minister." The man's eyes lighted up with interest and pleasure, and he asked, "Are you going to hold a meeting here?"

"I can't!" Al said. "The governor has prohibited all meetings. There is a ban on them."

Very earnestly the man insisted, "These people are dying! I live among them and I know them. Brother, they are *lost*! Hell waits for them if you don't tell them about Jesus. You *can't* pass by and refuse them the Word of Life!"

Greatly interested, Al asked, "Why don't *you* preach to them?"

Very sadly the man said, "Would to God I could! But I forfeited all right to that long ago. I also am lost!"

With great regret Al said, "Well, I'm sorry, but there is nothing I can do. I am dead on my feet, we have advertised no services, there is the governor's ban, and I am powerless."

Fiercely the man cried, "Regardless of the governor or any other earthly power, these poor souls must not perish! You *can't* refuse to let them know of Jesus."

Al surrendered. He rested for an hour, ate a hasty meal and repaired to the agreed place of meeting. The room was jammed to capacity, some of the audience being so sick and feeble they lay on the floor to listen. Al was still so tired that he preached seated in a chair, and had the deep joy of seeing some of the wretched shanty folk turn to Christ for salvation.

It was then too late to go on to the bed reserved for him, so he shared a rude pallet with two other men; fortunately not as huge as he himself was. He was asleep almost before he lay down, and exhaustion claimed his body. How long he lay there he never knew, nor could he afterward tell whether he was asleep and dreaming or was awake and had a vision. But suddenly he saw himself seated in a chair playing with a stalwart, healthy child. The youngster turned its head, and Al looked into the face of the babe he had prayed for that day, apparently much older.

When he awakened he hastened to the home, the joy of his dream or vision strong in him. He came to the sick mother, put his hand on her head and said, "Mother, just lie quietly and get well, your baby will recover. God has showed me He will answer our prayers, and the child will live."

The woman studied his face for a long minute, then she smiled and said, "Man of God, I believe you!" and she turned over to sleep peacefully. In later months Channer played with the child just as he had seen himself do in his dream. The degenerate preacher got a new grip on God and regained his faith, and afterward found a place of service in the woods that had sheltered him.

So the results of the Michigan Miracle were certainly *not* by might nor by power, because an exhausted, beaten man entered upon a task so hopeless only the Spirit of God could have carried it to a successful conclusion. He came to a moral morass and he left behind him men and women rejoicing in Christ, living in a renovated environment, determined to live on a level becoming to the children of God. The turning back of the Red Sea, the sending of manna from Heaven, the raising of Lazarus, and the feeding of the five thousand were no more miraculous than what God did in Michigan through His servant Al Channer, and no man can know of these episodes and doubt that God still lives and moves in the affairs of men.

The great north country is greatly changed today, but its challenge is just as impelling. The woods are still full of lumberjacks, but the conditions of their life are indifferent. Where the unending files of Norway pines once stood to offer quick wealth to the lumber barons, and where lusty men once took out great timbers, a second generation of woodsmen cut pulpwood, cedar posts and poles, and some pine for lumber where scattered stands still exist. Their lives are not nearly so isolated, since logging is now done by trucks to a great extent. But the same bitter blizzards blow, and the same hazards and temptations still exist. To offset these, the same man of God, the last of the giants, is still carrying the Word of God to them. Al Channer is now gray of hair, the proud possessor of nine grandchildren, but his powerful frame is still unbowed, and his great heart still beats in love for the people whom he calls "mine own."

On an average Sunday he preaches four times in four separate places, driving his car over backwoods roads an average of two hundred miles to finish his day's work. All alone he covers a parish which is two hundred sixty-four miles one way and two hundred and fifty-three miles the other. That is an area of sixty-six thousand square miles, which is a goodly territory for one man to ramble in! By auto alone he travels twenty-eight thousand miles a year to fulfill his preaching engagements. He buries the dead, marries the living, baptizes the babies and prays with the sick of this vast area, and conducts more than a score of revival meetings a year. With all of that he still finds time to keep up his ministry to the lumberjacks, and carry the knowledge of Jesus Christ to them.

His predecessor, John Sornberger, began a relief work to which Al fell heir, and he gathers and distributes tons of clothing to the needy in the backwoods and clearings. His car is an ambulance that is ever at the disposal of the sick, and his energy is unflagging in all good works.

For fifteen years he has conducted a summer camp for youngsters, under the authority of the Presbytery of Duluth, and in the face of conditions that would discourage anyone else, he has made it a great factor in the lives of many boys and girls who have little to remember. The one crop that never fails in the north is children, and some promising and stalwart lads and lassies dwell on the homesteads and in clearings. It is a pioneer existence, they are border folks, and live mostly by barter. Which means that cash is a stranger to most of them, so Channer runs the summer camp on the basis of $5.50 a week per person. That means that he has to gather and transport his staff and the children, feed them all three meals a day (and *such* meals these children can tuck away), pay all of his bills, and come out even at the rate of five dollars and fifty cents per person! But wait a minute before you say "it can't be done!" Many of these children come from poor homes, where five dollars is a huge sum. And when from three to six come from the same home, there just isn't that much money in one pioneer family's purse. So the children are permitted to pay half their camp cost in produce; any thing that can be eaten! This cuts down the cash income to a low level. I *know* it can't be done, but Channer does it year after year! The presbytery allows him the fabulous sum of fifty dollars a year to cover the rent of the camp–any deficit he is privileged to absorb himself. The salary of a missionary is pitifully small to begin with, and will not stand many such unexpected drains upon it. The astonishing fact is that the rate has never been raised in those fifteen years in spite of increasing costs and shrinking incomes.

But out of those camps have come missionaries, ministers of the Gospel, and consecrated Christian workers of all classes. Boys and girls have there found

Christ and a love for each other, and over the years Christian homes have dotted the frontier as a result of this effort.

We marvel how any man can survive under the load this man has borne for thirty-five years. He has been an authorized Sunday School Missionary, and has started some thirty-five Sunday Schools. The story of some of them deserve a chapter apiece, to tell of the hardships overcome and the great good accomplished. With all the rest of his labours, in the summer of 1947 Al Channer supervised twenty backwoods daily vacation Bible Schools, with the aid of one salaried assistant and four volunteer helpers. To keep them in the field, the Sky Pilot had to provide their board, in many instances acting as cook when there was no one else to feed and serve them.

Even iron wears out, and the toughest steel may become crystalized with age and much use. Nothing can stand continued strain without showing its effect, and the Rev. Elwyn Channer is also flesh and blood. Still manfully pursuing the course to which God ordained him, he wears the Mantle of the power of God in the ancient tradition. None of the giants who went before him have cause to regret that their Mantle fell upon this man. He walks with the same strides which marked their passage. He has won for himself a great place in the foremost ranks of those who serve God acceptably, but his years are limited.

Who shall catch the Mantle when it falls from his tired shoulders? Is there now being trained a man of the north who can follow this, the last of the giants? If there is, I know him not, but this I *do* know: There is always a Timothy to follow a Paul, "apostolic succession" cannot fail. The work is of God and the cause is His, and in His own good time He will raise up and call the next one to wear the Mantle. That day is not yet, years of service and fruitful toil stretch ahead of the iron man who now carries the light of the knowledge of Jesus Christ to homestead, clearing, logging camps, and mills, and the successor to his great work must be found by God, who alone can commission and ordain men to such a service as this.

*Finis*